THE WINTRY SEA

THE WINTRY SEA

Rupert Croft-Cooke

W. H. ALLEN
LONDON
1964

Printed in Great Britain by The Alden Press, Oxford
for the publishers W. H. Allen & Co., Essex Street, London W.C.2
Bound by G. & J. Kitcat Ltd., London S.E.1

Contents

1

THE ROCK

I have given this book its title because the words seem to fit each of the two journeys it records, journeys which, in the cant phrase of the courtroom, ran concurrently. The first was through the Mediterranean on a Yugoslav cargo boat during the coldest months of one of Europe's most icy winters for a century. The second was along the coastlines of some recent fiction. If I need another reason, the words are quoted from *The Schooner Hesperus* which was the first piece of horror fiction I read, for it chilled me at the age of seven.

For me the essential of a holiday is that its planning should be taken out of my hands and it is not merely facetious to say that the only real holiday in my life was provided by my six years in the army, when all decisions were made for me. Here it would be the same—the route decided by the exigencies of cargo, for passengers are a very small consideration on a ship like this, and my choice of fiction made for me by the booksellers in various ports on whose stocks of Penguins I should rely.

But a real holiday it was to be, a month or two of rest after several years of the overwork inevitable to one who enjoys it. A holiday with all its trappings, late rising, change of scenery, solitude, visits to unknown places, good food and drink and— as I thought—some light reading. If I had been going from England I should have added sunlight, but since I live in Tangier I could take my chance of this and was prepared for snow and crisp weather. All these things I hoped to find on a freighter running from Tangier to Yugoslavia and calling at a number of Italian and Sicilian ports. There would be no trains to catch, none of the fearful boredom of flying, no engagements to keep and no regrets at having missed something in the theatre or cinema, on television or radio. But a holiday also from the things I loved, the difficult but sometimes ecstatic gardening of Morocco, cooking, that most immediately rewarding of the arts, guests from England, motoring and *The Times* crossword. Clichés do not grow in the language without good reason and it is not for nothing that we speak of 'a nice change'.

Besides, the trip promised well. Gibraltar, not as I usually saw it on a hurried shopping excursion from Tangier but with a few days to see friends and equip myself for the journey. Then Savona, a port north of Genoa at which ships of the Yugoslav Line rarely called, Genoa itself a city I had never seen, Naples to which I, like most of its visitors, longed to return, Catania, Venice and Rijeka, once Fiume, where I could stay as long as I wished and from which I could visit other places in Yugoslavia.

The trip into fiction promised well, too, for it would be the first I had made for ten years since I reviewed for the *Sketch* and had to read all too many new novels. That was a curious job— a page to myself, my own choice of books at the *Sketch* offices, freedom to say what I liked and no editorial interference. It was not lavishly paid but the books themselves, sold to a useful functionary called a reviewer's bookseller, produced a monthly benefit free of income tax, and that made it worth while. But when I look back over the hundred and fifty odd Book Pages I did in those years I seem to have worked through an uninteresting epoch for with one or two exceptions no writer of significance emerged. On the contrary, it is depressing to find how many names loudly heralded by parental publishers are heard no more, and how many then bright and established reputations have been extinguished.

One of those exceptions was Angus Wilson. When *The Wrong Set*, his first book, and that a collection of short stories, came out in 1949 I 'ventured the prediction' that he had 'a notable future' as a writer, no very remarkable piece of foresight since his qualities should have been obvious to any wakeful critic, and when *Such Darling Dodos* was published a year later I made the mistake of asking for something on a more ambitious scale from an author who is really an inspired miniaturist. I also reviewed a first—or was it a second?—novel by Lawrence Durrell, issued by an obscure publisher in 1948 and uninvitingly called *Cefalu*. I thought Mr Durrell was clever, 'much too clever to be a good novelist or even a very good writer'. Moreover I seem to have let myself go on George Orwell's *Nineteen Eighty-four* and Oliver Onions's *Arras of Youth*, and kept to the fore, as well as I was able in that obscure corner of the critical world, names which were either taken for granted or forgotten elsewhere, Gerald Kersh, Jocelyn Brooke and William Sansom, Frederic Prokosch and Richard Llewellyn, who got a hostile press for a book called *A Few Flowers for Shiner* which I thought one of the best novels of army life I had read.

But there were no breathtaking discoveries during that time and little to console one for the grinding work, so at the end of it, when I had not once failed to send in my copy every other Monday for six years, I felt I should never want to read a new novel again, and for the rest of my life be satisfied with the books I knew and cared for, letting others perform that exhausting feat which is called 'keeping abreast of the time'.

But rumours reached me—even in Tangier. New names emerged with a fanfare and reputations were made overnight with something called the 'proletarian' novel—an odd form of categorization, I thought. I was told, as we all are, that I *must* read this or that, and adjectives, in the conversation of my friends, hummed like sirens. So-and-So was 'terrific', So-and-So 'important'. It was teasing and provocative and stirred the old curiosity and the old optimism which had made me open every parcel of books from the *Sketch* with hope. Now was the time to put it to the proof. My days at sea would be filled with novel reading and from it I might learn something of recent trends. This reading would be forced on me, for there would be nothing else to do, but it would be unprofessional and uncritical. Or so I thought.

2

As a young man I travelled on cargo boats because I could afford no other, but with the years I have found in them the happiest means of transport. I prefer the term tramp steamer, suggesting as it does haphazard wanderings from port to port, and one of the attractions of such a voyage is that the passenger does not know precisely where it will take him or how long it will last. Between ports may come a signal to the Captain that an extra call is to be made or even a new route followed. But a tramp steamer has other advantages over a liner, for the passenger. One is truly at sea, and not staying at a huge holiday camp, in motion over the remote irrelevant waves. One is among seamen who are the most interesting and interested beings alive, who never seem to lose their gusto or their humour and are tolerant and a little inquisitive in their attitude to landsmen, one of the few professions left in a hurried world whose marks are still distinguishable.

Then on a tramp steamer there are no appearances to be kept up, no vast amount of luggage to be brought for the voyage. One is emancipated not from good manners but from the fal-lals of civilization, a kind of freedom very precious to me. Moreover one is part of the life of the ship, one lives for a little while as seamen do with none of their obligations and responsibilities but nevertheless with them, eating in the officers' saloon and having the freedom of the ship. The food is lavish and simple with no phony gastronomic pretensions, with none of the liner's grandiose menus or would-be *haute cuisine*.

Again the passenger on a tramp steamer has longer in ports, time to explore or re-examine, not a hurried hour or two in which to find himself dragged to some urgent task of sightseeing. And he does not land in a large posse of tourists, the prey of pimps and souvenir salesmen, but wanders ashore with a few of the crew and sees the place as they see it, coming from the sea. I sometimes—fatuously, no doubt—think I could spend the rest of my life on cargo ships, moving from port to port and from one line to another, round the world or up and down it, lost for a year in the Antipodes or endlessly shambling about Asia or South America.

But for the man bound by time, tyrannized over by his calendar and wristwatch, this kind of travel has one distinct disadvantage, he cannot tell just when it is to begin and end. The ship *Trepča* on which I was to sail was due at Tangier from New York on a certain day, having left America at midnight on the eve of a docks strike, but she was delayed by storms in

[5]

the Atlantic. As I had arranged to leave my home on the Friday I did so, crossing to Gibraltar on the ferry to await the *Trepča* there, her first port of call after Tangier. In the event it was not till the Monday evening that I went aboard, having passed three days on the Rock.

But I have the faculty of giving a psychological twist to the events of my own life and so could start my holiday when I left my home, seeing Gibraltar, which I have visited as a shopping-centre scores of times in the last nine years, as the first port on my journey.

3

In theory Gibraltar is a romantic place, an outpost, a fortress and a last fragment of the colonial empire. In fact the only Gibraltar seen by the public is a hillside on which cluster a few flea-bitten Barbary apes and a street of shops many of them displaying the shoddy bits of ill-carved ivory, the Japanese cotton goods and valueless souvenirs which are the stock-in-trade of Indian commerce everywhere abroad. The hotels are cramped and old-fashioned without being picturesque, the population the descendants of nineteenth-century settlers from Spain, Italy and Malta with two or three thousand Jews who form a distinct society of their own. The people speak no language perfectly, both Spanish and English being fluent but incorrect and full of local colloquialisms. They are friendly and cheerful folk, insistent on their British citizenship. It is hard to associate the isthmus now with its lurid history or its magnificent resistance to the sieges and attacks, alarms from the sea and land which beset it for eighty years after Rooke appropriated it in 1704. At first, it appears, we were prepared to con-

[6]

sider its restitution to the Spanish crown and twice there were diplomatic exchanges to bring it about, but by 1720 sentiment at home had become adamant against surrendering it.

That is all that remains today of those struggles and negotiations with their tragic casualties—the staunchness of British public opinion that the Rock must never be given up. It is a strange survival in an age of abandonment. Strategically useless, economically an encumbrance, Gibraltar unites every political creed in a chorus of *No pasaran*, and there is a revival of Victorian imperialism in every breast when restitution is even suggested. Faced with the question 'How would *you* like it if the Isle of Wight were a Spanish or French possession through an error of warfare two hundred and fifty years ago?' the Englishman becomes inarticulate with rage. Nor does the Spanish case receive any support from the Gibraltarians or from the thousands of Spaniards whose living depends on continued British occupation.

Yet the story of Gibraltar, which has yet to be written in all its fullness, is an exciting and highly coloured one. A cave excavated during the last war revealed four levels of occupation from Neanderthal to Roman times and as one of the Pillars of Hercules, Mons Calpe, it marked the limit to all reasonable seafaring endeavour of the ancient world. It owes its present name to its Arab conqueror of A.D. 711 Tarik ibn Zaid, being called Jebel Tarik, Mount Tarik, after him. Some of his fortifications, including a massive square tower known as the Moorish Castle, still stand. In 1309 the Spaniards recovered it from the Moors but twenty-four years later these won it back and it was part of the domain of the Moorish ruler of Granada till 1462 when it became Spanish once more till our own forces occupied it in 1704.

Thereafter the fighting till 1783 was spasmodic but intense. Regarded as a point at issue which no home government dared to ignore, Gibraltar could be defended against almost any attack but not without casualties, and in remembering this, as any colonial warfare, it is difficult to forget the young men from English counties, illiterate, fed with crude propaganda of loyalty to King and Country (which served as late as 1914–18), recruited from a poverty-driven and often hungry peasantry, brought here by troopships with conditions little better than those of African slave-traders, flogged for indiscipline, set on the Rock to scorch and thirst and often to die for no good reason but the protection of our Mediterranean and East Indian trade, a cause which could have made no great appeal to even the most intelligent of them. Three months after Rooke had run up the British flag (though the Rock had been seized in the name of the Archduke Charles of Austria) the Spanish and French began their first siege which lasted six months and failed because of the fierce resistance of Admiral Sir John Leake and Prince George of Hesse-Darmstadt, so that at the Treaty of Utrecht in 1713 Spain acknowledged England's title. In 1773, however, began one of the most memorable sieges in all history, lasting for ten years. The Spaniards blockaded the isthmus from the land side, constructing siege batteries under fire from the fortress. The privateer *Buck* forced her way into the harbour with supplies, but not until 1780 did Admiral Sir George Rodney win a naval victory and enter with a convoy. The Spaniards attacked unsuccessfully with fire ships but did not open up with their shore batteries till the next year when a British relieving squadron under Admiral Darby arrived and stores were landed under heavy bombardment, which continued spasmodically till a sortie, made on the night of November 26th, 1781, destroyed most of the Spanish fortifications. Next April the Governor had the foresight to order grates for heating shot, and when the grand attack came, and ten ships specially constructed with green timber fortified six or seven feet thick, bolted with iron, cork and raw hides, took up their positions in daylight, it was only red-hot shot which saved the garrison. One by one each of the ten ships was set on fire in a battle which continued into the night and the scene both on shore and afloat must have been infernal, for more than 8300 rounds were expended by the garrison from less than a hundred pieces of artillery. Another naval victory, this time by Admiral Lord Howe, clinched the matter and the Treaty of Versailles (1780) once more confirmed Britain's possession of the Rock which remained publicly unquestioned till recent Spanish propaganda has attempted to revive the issue. That almost the whole civil population of Gibraltar was evacuated during the last war I knew, for I served in the army with two of the men chosen for a Field Security Section for their knowledge of Spanish.

But all that derring-do of Gibraltarian history was far from my mind as I came ashore from the *Mons Calpe* that January afternoon and commenced my weeks of holiday.

4

Not too comfortably, however. Most of the hotels were already full and I found myself in a grim half-furnished bedroom of one of the nastier taverns with the pretensions and title of a hotel. Its gimmick was to charge for one meal with a night's lodging—'We don't *do* the bed and breakfast,' said a po-faced young woman at the desk—and because I was tired and unenterprising I weakly went in to dinner which was of course uneatable.

But I was rewarded afterwards by hearing in the hotel lounge a very extraordinary conversation between two competing bores, each of whose wives sat by in silence. Were these women inured to the humdrum pomposities of the men they had been forced to live with and listen to for many years? Or were they still dazed with admiration at their husbands' loquacity? Neither of them uttered.

The talk began with tentative exchanges on the immediate circumstances and activities of the two, and I gathered that one was a doctor from New Zealand enjoying a well-deserved holiday to be spent motoring in Europe.

The other gave me my first shock.

'We've been here eight months now. Retired here, you might say.'

Eight months! Up and down that dreary street of shops. Once a week to look at the apes scratching themselves. The servicemen had nervous breakdowns from sheer boredom in the place. How could anyone retire to it? But more incredible was to come.

'We've lived in this hotel from the start, as a matter of fact.'

I had to pretend to great puzzlement over my crossword, but the New Zealander found nothing remarkable in this confession.

'It seems very nice,' he said pulling out his pipe.

'Suits us,' said the elder man. 'Good plain food. We don't like a lot of made-up dishes. We should have liked a room with a bathroom but there's one just at the end of the passage.'

The New Zealander nodded understandingly.

'Plenty of hot water?'

'Usually, yes. It's not luxurious of course. But we're not luxury-loving people. We find it most interesting here. Different people almost every night.'

So that was it. Every evening a new interlocutor. The New Zealander who had been filling his pipe abstractedly was

[10]

clearly preparing to make a pronouncement, perhaps when he had lit it. I have noticed that pipes go with some of the most entertaining talk and also with some of the most dismally flat and ponderous. Sir Compton Mackenzie smokes a pipe and is perhaps the greatest conversationalist since the eighteenth century, but also every one of those long-chinned, long-toothed, long-winded men whom one can recognize as the most resolute of bores before they speak, every savant of cricket, every owner of a remarkable dog or motor car, every narrator of 'an extraordinary dream I had last night', pulls comfortably at a pipe while he is torturing you.

'I often think . . .' came out at last between puffs, before some excruciating platitudes.

'I always say . . .' riposted the other gallantly, not to be out-done.

'By and large . . .' said the New Zealander.

'In my considered opinion . . .' began the Englishman after hearing him out.

'I was only saying to the wife . . .'

'I read in the paper the other day . . .'

'As a matter of actual fact . . .'

'I wouldn't go so far as to suggest . . .'

There I must have lost touch for the moment for when my attention had returned they had found the topic most admirably suited to their talents—the Common Market. The New Zealander had something to say about that in a manner between man-to-man and after-dinner-speech, slowly, pointedly, mercilessly, each sentence driven in like a coffin-nail by a mighty pause and a pipe puff, each commonplace sentiment mouthed with sickening self-satisfaction.

'We in New Zealand . . . rather pride ourselves . . . on being second to none . . . in loyalty to the Crown . . . but this Common Market thing . . . has come as a shock to us.'

B

The Englishman nodded. The two wives continued staring into space. Did they even hear?

'You see, we don't forget. At the end of the war . . . I remember it as though it were yesterday . . . our Prime Minister appealed to us . . . to continue rationing . . . so that we could help the Old Country with supplies. We did so quite cheerfully . . . but now . . . well, we don't forget, that's all . . .'

'I see your point,' claimed the Englishman. 'But . . .'

'Not that we regret it . . . I daresay we should do the same again . . . but I think the British should realize . . . before they rush into the Common Market . . . how we feel.'

I have noticed that the Common Market to its critics was always something to be 'rushed into', never entered with deliberation. The Englishman made another attempt to mount.

'What you say is very interesting because . . .'

But the New Zealander was firmly in the saddle.

'Mind you, if I were in Macmillan's place . . . I'm not at all sure . . . that I wouldn't do the same thing . . . I don't quite see . . . what else he can do. But the people where I come from . . . can't be expected to see it like that.'

'No. No. Quite. But just for the sake of argument . . .'

This time he was up. There was another half hour of give-and-take with no more solo oratory, which I sincerely regretted. Not since I sat under H. R. Stokoe at Tonbridge had I known quite such excruciating sententiousness and I would have liked a little, though a very little, more.

It was time for bed.

'Well, I've enjoyed our little chat,' said the Englishman.

'Most interesting.'

'You off in the morning?'

'Yes, we thought we'd spend a night at Torremolinos.'

'Very nice place.'

'See you at breakfast, perhaps?'
'Yes. Certainly. We always come down for it.'
'Well, it's been very nice to meet you.'
'Very nice. Very interesting.'
'We'll say good night, then.'
'Good night. Hope you don't find it too noisy.'
'Not a bit. Sleep like a top. Good night.'
Suddenly both wives seemed to wake.
'Good night,' each said with a smile.
'Good night, then.'
'Good night.'
'Good night.'

5

Next day I lunched with Darrell and Susan Bates. In the context I should perhaps say that Darrell is the Colonial Secretary in Gibraltar, but for me he is a writer and the first who has turned the life in far places of a colonial administrator into first-rate entertainment.

To leave the stuffy Main Street and my shoddy hotel and climb high among the trees and rocks where a few houses for government officials have pleasant gardens and splendid outlooks is to remember the colonial system of other centuries, the cantonments of India where cool sahibs lived under punkahs half a mile from the crawling bazar, or the 'Residences' scattered about the Pacific and the East with smart little brown sentries at their gates. Darrell's home is called a cottage, but it is imposing enough to have a great reception room on the ground floor, shuttered and used only for official occasions or a teenagers' dance, when a huge scuffle of the friends of Darrell's

[13]

sons and daughter take it over for the evening, uninvigilated by adults.

There is nothing exotic about the household, however. Two young Sherburnians with wild manes and English good manners, with a sister as energetic as they, were planning a fishing expedition to which Susan their mother was being pressingly invited. A cheerful family lunch—masses of shellfish and mayonnaise—and Darrell himself, his white poll failing to give solemnity to his young face, talking not of Gibraltar or the problems of civil administration in such a mixed population, but talking of royalties (authors', not visiting), of contracts and publishers, 'shop' more interesting to a writer than literary movements or tendencies. Yet this was Gibraltar, at another level physically and in thought from the market-place of a town I had left below, no less an outcome of those early efforts to hold the Rock, very English, modern and delightful.

Down again to the babel of Main Street, but determined not to spend more nights in that hotel, I called on another friend who promptly saved me from them by the offer of a room in his flat.

Twenty odd years ago Hudson Smith had shared with me the bizarre experience of undergoing training in Field Security at a requisitioned theological college in Winchester, but whereas for me I.B. and all its anomalies had been a wartime occupation, Hudson made it his profession and holds some security post on the Rock, bringing a humorous and mature mind to it. A friend of writers, Colin MacInnes among them, he knew Hemingway, collects books, loves wine, Spain and music. He has a civilized fruity character and is one of the comparatively few human beings in these regions with whom it is tolerable to spend a long evening in conversation, though not without the usually welcome interruptions of his charmingly loquacious and hospitable wife Margaret.

[14]

When I had moved my bags to his flat in Irish Town, a narrow alley running parallel to Main Street, and drunk successively two cups of tea and a whisky and soda, I heard that we were to cross the frontier to the Spanish town of La Linea.

'We have promised to go to Elizabeth's,' said Margaret. She gave no further explanation, but something in that, her assumption that I should know whom she meant, the Christian name used alone, the happy anticipation in her voice, led me to expect an unusual human being, home, or evening, and in none was I disappointed.

Born a Russian, Elizabeth Creswell was untamed by years of marriage to an English diplomat and remained Chekovian, vivid, impulsive, almost violent in speech, having all that I, who know Russians from their novels, expect to find in them. Her house round an open patio was full of small beautiful things haphazardly arranged and depleted, one imagined, by break-ages that had caused tears or laughter. Handsome, restless, like a flame, like gypsy music, like a storm, Elizabeth moved, talked, half-listened, hurried out, returned, sat for a moment, jumped up, poured drinks, all with a light energetic grace. She was expecting her son who was on some crazy drive through rain into the mountains in an open car with three young friends. He was late. Or was he late? Nobody seemed to know the time.

It was so like *The Cherry Orchard* that when we were taken to call briefly on Elizabeth's mother and found a beautiful old Russian woman propped up in bed, white-haired, *ancien régime* but very keenly aware of the present, this whole piece of Slav fiction could scarcely have been more according to the precedents.

When Elizabeth's son arrived with two young house surgeons and a nurse from a Gibraltar hospital, all drenched to the skin, one shoeless from a misfortune by the way, talkative and hungry, confusion and laughter rose and kept a high pitch. It was suddenly necessary that we should all eat. How many? It did not matter how many. There were *lentejas*. Lentil stew. Enough for us all. And plenty of wine. Olives, too. There were olives and *salchichas* and cheese. This caused a new stir. Elizabeth disappeared for a time. The young people dried themselves. More drinks. Then we were all round a table eating lentil stew.

'*Lentejas*!' quoted Elizabeth's polyglot son. '*Si las quieres, las tomas—y si no, las dejas.*'

The vast cauldron brought to the table was soon emptied. Cheese? More wine? Talk which ran like a tide. Laughter. Things suddenly remembered with a cry. Chekov could not have done it better.

Finished? We must go to the Zorongo! We must *all* go to the Zorongo, a bar in La Linea. Flamenco music. It would be crowded tonight, Saturday, but never mind.

Crowded it was, with a strange helter-skelter of English tourists and a circle of Spaniards. The waiter danced. There was nowhere to sit and Spanish abandon suddenly seemed rather tame and tired after that Russian household.

6

Next day I met a splendid old character named Hope-John-son, the dedicatee of one of Compton Mackenzie's books who had been with him during the First World War and spoke of Mackenzie, with some emphasis, as 'Celtic'. He had been acquainted with Robert Ross and said that More Adey was known as 'the Bearded Lady'. He talked brilliantly and long of

Monty Mackenzie and the early days of *The Gramophone* with which he had been associated, of his friend Roger Fry and Archibald Marshall. He was not prosy and as young in spirit as Mackenzie himself whose birthday was four days before his.

But on Monday I learned that the *Trepča* was in at last and that I must embark that afternoon.

2

THE *TREPČA*

I went out to the *Trepca* on the agent's launch. To board a vessel this way seems a decisive move to make— one is leaving one kind of life for another. Merely to step aboard when the ship is alongside the docks is to pass from a stone surface to a metal or wooden one, entering a ship rather than boarding her. Or so it has always seemed to me.

The agent took me to the Captain's cabin where I was formally greeted by a hearty deep-voiced bear of a man. This, though I was unaware of it, was the only time I should speak to the Captain or any of his officers and men with the exception of the Chief Steward, during my five weeks aboard. Although the ship's company were impeccably courteous and saluted and greeted passengers when they met, fraternization with those from capitalist countries was forbidden. We had separate saloons, unlike all the friendly cargo boats on which I had travelled. The Captain and many of his officers spoke excellent English, but they said no more than good morning and good night.

[*18*]

This was somewhat daunting to a man as gregarious as I, and when I learnt that afternoon that my only fellow-passenger would be a deportee from America, a young Yugoslav who had emigrated as a small boy and was now being sent back for involvement in petty crime and immigration offences, I saw that there would be some solitary weeks ahead in which I would be dependent on the stock of Penguins I had bought in Gibraltar.

But the Chief Steward was a consolation. An oldish man who had been at sea since boyhood he had a sad kindly smile, spoke some English, dyed his hair a dark auburn and treated me with the humorous tolerance which seamen often show to passengers coming aboard. My bags were brought up from the agent's launch, tea was produced and I was told that my fellow-passenger would appear for dinner at half-past six. Half-past six? Yes. The officers dined at six, the passengers half an hour later. It was the last meal of the day.

I examined my cabin, an old-fashioned compartment with mahogany-framed bunks one above the other. I saw that there were three saloons, a dining saloon for passengers and a bare room with shabby curtains and some battered chessmen in a cupboard which was also intended for passengers though I never afterwards entered it, and the officers' saloon. All were empty and needed new curtains and re-upholstering.

But I was determined not to feel depressed and when I had unpacked, I searched through my Penguins for something to read, something which would, in a popular phrase, take me out of myself. I wondered a little fatuously whether my own books took people out of themselves. I hoped so. It is, crudely expressed, what is to be demanded of a novelist—and rightly so. I picked up *Under the Net* by Iris Murdoch.

The name of this writer had become familiar to me in the last few years, for even in Tangier we see the *Sunday Times* and the *Observer* and a good deal of their reviewing space has recently been devoted to her. A new kind of thriller-writer, wasn't she? She was, I noted from the blurb of another book, placed by *The Times Literary Supplement* 'in the front rank of British novelists writing today', but that old front rank stretches out so widely that I was not much encouraged by this. And when I began to read *Under the Net* I was not encouraged at all, for it started as any thriller might since Dashiell Hammett— 'When I saw Finn waiting for me at the corner of the street I knew at once that something had gone wrong.'

But it was worse than this promised. It wasn't a thriller at all. There was not a corpse waiting or a lot of bad men round that corner. Finn was a comedy Irishman and the whole book, I soon realized, was written with a determination to be funny. Or as the blurb said—'both entertaining in a Marx Brothers way and moving as tragedy'.

After a hundred pages of it, including six of slapstick business with a performing dog, I fell into the sad reflection that (in English, at all events) there has not been a female comic writer. Jane Austen is an exception to most rules but not really to this; delicious, salty, gently satirical, one says of her, not blatantly comic as Shakespeare or Dickens could be. Comic writing, as such, is a profession into which women have not yet infiltrated, like the Church and the Stock Exchange. As writers they are witty—wittier perhaps than men—they have a rich and lively sense of humour, they can bring tears to male eyes, but never tears of laughter. Subtle and swift and quick to see the uses of the grotesque, they have still not created any character to be thought of with Falstaff, Mrs Malaprop, Mr Micawber or

Huckleberry Finn, or any situation uproariously, vulgarly, wildly funny. No doubt all this will be remedied, and it can only be a question of time before there is a female Sterne and a female Wodehouse, but it has not happened yet. As a horse-laugh is indelicate in women, so a real guffaw, Rabelaisian or Dickensian, is not to be found in all their written work. When it is attempted the result is unhappy.

As it is in this book of Miss Murdoch's. With the best will in the world it is impossible to split one's sides over Jake Donaghue and Finn, Mrs Tinckham, Hugo Belfounder and the rest, because their creator is so relentlessly determined that one shall do so, and will sacrifice anything for a laugh. Even her lovely young women are made funny before they are credible with the result that they are neither.

As I read on—and of course I *did* read on for Miss Murdoch is intelligent and sometimes shrewd—I became conscious of an undertone, a strange little noise audible all the time. I could not account for it for a while then realized it was the author, chuckling away to herself with every sentence she wrote. What, I asked uncomfortably, was she laughing at? Not her characters or herself. Not her situations or her dialogue. No, it was at the reader, stumbling on with a real wish to believe in her people, wanting things to turn out right for them, being such an ass as to take any interest in them at all.

It was not for her characters that Miss Murdoch had laid her banana skin, but for me. And I slipped on it straight away. I hoped Jake would get out of his difficulties, or somebody find more than a night's happiness with someone else, only at the end to hear the author saying: 'Sucks to you. They're only there for a laugh, and you've been trying to believe in them! Yah!'

Under the Net was not very entertaining, then, and certainly was not 'moving as tragedy'. But it had fooled me for a time and I was glad I had another Iris Murdoch novel with me. A

[21]

few days later I read *The Bell*, and began to discover what all
the critical fuss had been about.

For here, instead of trying to be funny, the author tries not
to be, and cannot help it, so that the humour, cool and refreshing, bubbles up again and again. The theme of the novel
is somewhat brackish, which makes this Attic spring more
welcome. Perhaps all humorists should be so against their own
inclination, as it were, certainly not by their own efforts.

Though *The Bell* is modern enough in treatment, it is
planned in a manner popular in the 1930s to embrace a small
community, each member of which has a story and a character,
the whole thing an intricate interplay of past histories, emotions,
reactions, with the various climaxes working up to one climax
and altogether too much plot. Admittedly this is not uncomfortably obvious, the joists are not visible to the naked eye and
the climax is not a bang-bang-bang explosion to obliterate any
loose ends. But the book is over-constructed.

The characters are all right. They have the right number of
dimensions and are recognizable not only as faces and bodies
(their bodies by no means neglected) but as intelligent units of
desire, ambition, regret and all the rest of it. People, in other
words. I can't think of a more successful portrayal of a nice
silly slapdash woman than Dora Greenfield and the reader soon
understands her better than her husband does.

An essential part of the theme is homosexuality and this is
usually a dull subject in fiction. Except for *Vestal Fire*, *Extraordinary Women* and James Baldwin's *Giovanni's Room* no one
has made from it anything but dreary intense studies in self-
immolation, and queer American novels read like Fox's *Book of
Martyrs*.

In *The Bell* there are two homosexuals and one embryo one,
all males. I did not quite believe in them but at least I was
forced to a grudging 'could be', which had never been wrung

from me before by one of these fictional portraits of queers. Michael's mixture of awareness and repression is suspect. Nick's particular kind of bitterness is over-dramatized, for given his circumstances he would have taken to writing or painting or become someone in television and soon have laughed it off. As for Toby, if the author supposes for a moment that he is not queer and going to be queerer she has missed her own point.

I was disappointed then. Here was one reputation, I reflected as I finished the second of Iris Murdoch's books, which had come into being since I had last read fiction, so that one of my chances of discovering for myself a new enthusiasm among emergent writers had vanished.

I began picking through *The Bell* again, reading bits here and there as though I might find some merit tucked like a bookmark between its pages. But this was unfair and when I had come on 'odiferous bath-salts' and 'a kaleidoscope of rippling skirts and flashing thighs' I desisted.

It was such a *novel*. Theme, plot, characterization, action and perhaps a mite of symbolism not too obviously introduced, all rounded off neatly and having a nice quiet sequel to the climax. It invited comparison not with shoddier novels of today but with those of forty years ago when the novel form seemed capable of everything and gave scope to writers as varied as Wells and E. M. Forster, Bennett and D. H. Lawrence. Yet its failure in that comparison might well be in my mind, just as the experiences of adolescence are brilliantly clear and remain for the rest of life, so reading was an adventure into bright new countries, every contour of which becomes idealized. A young man reading this book today might well find in it what I found in *Fiery Particles* or *The Longest Journey*. I did not really believe that, I admitted ruefully, but should I not give the author the benefit of the doubt? It was an intelligent book, anyway, and had kept its hold on me.

[23]

3

I needed a drink half-way through *Under The Net* and at the same time as my whisky and soda, arrived the deportee.

His name, he said, was Boris. He was small with somewhat simian features and looked as though he had to shave twice a day and have his hair cut once a week. He at once gave me his life-story. At thirteen he had run away from an unhappy and penurious home and crossed the frontier into Greece where he had told a tale of political persecution. He had lived for some weeks with Greek shepherds but had been found by refugee organizations and kept in a series of camps for some years until a passage had been arranged for him to the United States. He spoke in a thick slobby almost incomprehensible way, the language used in films by illiterate American gangsters. He could not read or write much English and his pronunciation was based on the faulty phonetics of New York slums.

'A worrange,' he said when I asked him what he would like to drink, though he changed this to a beer.

There was a long involved story of what had got him into trouble. He had been with 'dese guys' before they had robbed a shop and had come before the 'Junile Court'. He had married when he was seventeen a girl of fifteen and a half and that was against him, too. Well, not married exactly but they had a baby. He did not like Americans, he said. Why not? They had no manners and they wasn't *sin*cere. No, sir. Not *sin*cere at all.

They were good to him on this ship, though. Did I know the Captain might have kept him locked in his cabin all the time? He wasn't allowed ashore, of course, but they didn't lock him up. That was the Captain's sponsability. The Captain was good to him. 'I don't think there's no better man than this Captain.'

[24]

He asked me nothing for a long time, a form of rough good manners, I suspected. But presently he looked at me inquisitively several times before coming out with the question on his mind.

'Are you a miniollaire?' he asked with some awe.

When I realized what he meant I denied it with some emphasis and amusement and asked him what had made him think that. He looked rather embarrassed.

'I don't know. I just thought you might be a miniollaire. Some of the boys says you was.'

It was clearly a disappointment to him.

'But you're miniollaire class?' he pleaded.

Not even that, I told him, and tried to explain that degrees of wealth, even today in England, were not the only yardstick to apply to a man's life. There was happiness, for instance, freedom, and good health. This explanation fell very flat.

'If I was wealthy . . .' he began, and for a while said no more. I prompted him. 'I'd look for things. What you call that? A man who looks in the earth for old things? Stone and gold and that?'

'You mean an archaeologist?'

'Yeah. That's it. That's what I'd do.'

Too promptly at half-past six the Chief Steward brought dinner, a good ship's soup, vast slices of veal, green beans from the deep freeze, a beautiful but tasteless apple. I had lunched at two and could eat almost nothing but Boris made up for me.

'Ah was a cook in the States,' he explained.

'Oh. What did you cook?'

'Steaks. Nearly all steaks. They didn't seem to eat much else where I was cooking.'

Liquor could be bought only by the bottle on that ship, even spirits and liqueurs. The Chief Steward recommended a Yugoslav cherry brandy and I remembered hearing from a man of taste in drink that it was the finest in the world. He was right, I

[25]

think now. Fruitier, more spirituous yet richer than the Danish, it serves as an accompaniment to coffee and a cigar. I am not a liqueur enthusiast but I bought a bottle and enjoyed it on those few occasions on the voyage when the meal demanded such a sweetmeat.

Afterwards I went on deck. The moon, like the one seen from the schooner *Hesperus*, had a silver ring. We had not left our moorings and the lights of Gibraltar and La Linea shone in hazy yellow festoons. The outline of the huge Rock was black and portentous against the sky and there was silence. Tomorrow we should sail.

4

Next morning was wet and misty and though we had not moved, the Rock was out of sight. In this dull cold weather I wanted to read something reliable, something comfortingly good that would not only 'take me out of myself' but 'carry me away'. On board I had not many books already known to me, but among the Penguins I saw, bound in grey to denote a 'modern classic', Aldous Huxley's *Those Barren Leaves*. 'The background of this sophisticated novel is sunny Italy' I read in the blurb, shivering at the grey sea and cold rain about me.

Huxley's early books, *Crome Yellow*, *Antic Hay*, *Little Mexican*, are a part of the youth of my generation, are remembered aspects of the 1920s rather than novels, as Noel Coward's numbers are remembered experiences rather than songs. We read Huxley's books as they came out and kept them in their dust-wrappers because before long they would be valuable first editions. We never had any doubt that Aldous Huxley would be *our* novelist, as Hardy, Wells and Galsworthy had been those of the generations before ours. About D. H. Lawrence we disputed but there was no argument about Huxley. As the blurb of *Mortal Coils* quotes from Cyril Conolly 'witty, serious, observant, well-read, sensitive, intelligent, there can have been few young writers as gifted as Huxley'. None, we cried, back in the twenties. When this man develops, as assuredly he will, and drops what we called (most unfairly for it was far more than that) his undergraduate cleverness, there will be nothing to stop him, and this age, *our* age, will have its Great Writer. Underneath the sparkling and sardonic manner we discerned a Big Heart. Not, we said patronizingly, like that of Dickens—there would never be a Huxleyan Little Nell—but nevertheless deep feeling conveyed with an engaging shrug, pathos behind the epigrams, and later perhaps real tragedy bursting through the elegant façade of the prose. There would be everything.

How we all envied him, we who were trying to write fiction in the twenties and thirties. So knowing, so *soigné*, so travelled, so inventive. We did not try to write like him, recognizing a unique and inimitable manner, but we felt, particularly the unacademic amongst us, an admiring jealousy of a writer only a decade or so older than us who could make us feel like schoolboys writing essays. Those conversations that filled his books, the sweep and wisdom of them, the wicked humour in his situations, the occasional broken heart tucked away neatly under smart clothes and smarter repartee. Just wait, we said, just wait till he gets into his stride.

When, I wonder now, did the first doubts begin to trouble us? Perhaps with *Point Counter Point* which *looked* so much like the book we had been expecting but seemed, as we read it, just a mite like the earlier books, written with wider scope, of course, at greater length, but not really getting anywhere. Or at least not getting where—and here I had better drop the presumptuous 'we'—not getting where I, at an eager twenty-five

c

years, wanted it to get, into the realms of what I still called great literature. It was a development, but it was not the development, And was that brilliance becoming just a little (dared I think it?) slick?

Brave New World could of course be admired without regret or reserve as a *tour de force*, something written by the way, highly intelligent and worth reading, but quite unindicative of the future which was still bright. Then *Eyeless in Gaza*. Then that glorious, macabre, disturbing joke *After Many a Summer*. (What splendid titles Huxley has always had. That superlative is certainly his—the best title-maker of them all.)

And then? What then? Frightfully interesting things. Experiments in some sort of Yogi, one heard, records of the benign influence of a drug, and a good deal of philosophical and historical and literary sagacity, but never what we were promised forty years ago, novels that would make the early books mere preludes to achievement. Never even the one novel that would show them to have been the glorious try-outs we thought them.

Well, well; let's be thankful for what we have and it is, after all, a very great deal. If Huxley is not a great novelist—that word great again—he is certainly a great writer and can use words with more assurance and éclat than anyone living. And readable? Just pick up *Those Barren Leaves* as I had done in a Tangier bookshop, and start reading it, as I did that ugly morning off Gibraltar, and you will see whether Huxley is readable.

We of the generation just after his were asking too much, that is all. It is a damned impertinence to plan what one thinks should be a writer's future, to demand a certain kind of achievement from him. Enough that one is able to return to each of his books with relief and pleasure as soon as it has become once more unfamiliar, and never be disappointed.

[*28*]

The last of our cargo from America was being discharged into lighters—a few million cigarettes in special cartons known as the Tangier Pack. This has been created for the benefit of smugglers operating from Tangier and Gibraltar. Each case of 10,000 cigarettes has first carton, then a special nylon covering, then carton again. It saves from immediate damage cases accidentally dropped into the sea when cargoes are being hurriedly transferred.

In my years of living in Tangier I have learned a good deal about smuggling, for although most of it is now done from Gibraltar, Tangier is by tradition the smugglers' port. Now and again some startling story circulates, as when a young English wife had to hurry to a Vigo hospital because her husband, a skipper of a ship carrying goods up the Spanish coast, had been taken ashore after being shot in the lung and stomach. His ship had been spotted by a Fishery Patrol vessel and ordered to stop. When this order was disobeyed the patrol vessel opened fire. The Englishman recovered in that case and was released on bail so that he could leave the country but never return to it.

Smuggling was quick to replace piracy on the Barbary Coast and has flourished ever since Mediterranean countries attempted to impose excise duties, but it only became big business after the Second World War when France, Spain and Italy, all countries with a tobacco monopoly, had empty shops, few dollars and a craving for cigarettes, nylons, whisky. At the same time Naval Disposals in England put on the market surplus Fairmile coastal patrol vessels at about £2000 each and with deserters still apprehensive and men finding civilian life unrewarding and unadventurous, the thing became a ramp. It cost about £5000 to buy a boat and make it ready for sea,

[29]

but with any luck that sum and more could be made by a single trip to Italy.

When the contraband trade from Tangier was at its peak in the years 1948–52 there were as many as seventy-five ships working full time and they were a serious threat to the economy of the Mediterranean area. The number has been reduced by more efficient shore patrols and improved economic conditions in Italy and Spain but there are still ten to fifteen contraband ships based on Tangier and a great many more in Gibraltar. All of them are registered under the British flag for traditionally the British uphold the right of High Seas Trading or the transfer of a cargo at sea, while all Mediterranean countries are against this. Also, only the British, and one or two central American republics, allow ships of under 200 tons to carry a cargo of tobacco.

Gibraltar has become the principal loading centre. There is no difficulty about this and a blind eye is turned to the destination given for cargoes of cigarettes which is always put down on the cargo manifest as 'Malta'. If statistics were worked out on this basis it would be seen that for the past twenty years every man, woman and child in Malta has been smoking more than a thousand cigarettes a day.

The profits are still enormous. A Fairmile from which everything has been removed to make room for cargo can carry 2000 cases of 10,000 cigarettes each. These cost, with all shore expenses in Tangier, 43 dollars a case packed on board. Ashore in Italy they will make 100 dollars a case and in Spain about 75. It will be seen that a successful trip to Italy means a gross profit of something like 100,000 dollars to be divided between the various parties.

Spain, however, is still short of everything that costs dollars or sterling and the smugglers have taken to running mixed cargoes to her shores. Very often orders for specific goods are taken, sometimes for a back axle or a quantity of copper wire. Recently a beneficent smuggler carried 450 bales of hops to Spain for a desperate brewer who had waited too long for an import licence. Even wireless sets are sent ashore and the sales of whisky have been raised considerably.

The contrabandists do not break the laws of Morocco or of Great Britain when they load in Tangier or Gibraltar. They are taking on such a cargo for such a destination; it is no affair of the port authorities what they may do with it later. In fact, if when the cargo is transferred to the ship sent out by the shore organization while both are outside the territorial waters of the country for which it is destined, the Tangier smuggler has not broken any law at all and is entitled to all the protection which the British flag gives him.

Far less was the Yugoslav Line guilty of an irregularity in carrying huge quantities of tobacco from America. But as I watched case after case of Marlboro cigarettes being swung over to the lighters I wondered how the population of Gibraltar would feel if they were expected to absorb even this one cargo of a particular brand.

It seemed only a few minutes after the last lighter had put back to shore that we sailed .The air was icy cold and the sea as smooth as though it were frozen.

3

AT SEA

I began to grow lonely. In the saloon Boris watched me with glassy violet eyes, fixed and greedy like a bird's. I realized that he had no money and amid all the plenty displayed while the cargo was unloaded had been without cigarettes. I bought him a carton but when he tried to repay me by more of his story—he had learned that I was not a 'miniollaire' but a writer—I discouraged him. He had a deep soft voice and had learnt English from semi-illiterate American teenagers no more articulate than he. That would not have mattered if he had a story to tell but it had all become a blur of odd jobs in hot kitchens, wild rides on motor-cycles, rooms shared with women, police stations and juvenile courts, and later immigration officers. Nothing vivid remained.

The prospect of three days at sea while we made for the Italian coast would have been unpromising if it were not for my pile of books now diminished by three. Perhaps for the first time in my life I realized what books can mean to people cut off from others by inclination or circumstances, to prisoners, to the blind, or to those in hospital. I saw that I had never been for more than an hour or two with 'nothing to do but read' and had read for pleasure or as a job, but never from absolute necessity.

I picked up William Golding's *Lord of the Flies* and was at once absorbed.

I knew nothing of the author, and of the book only that it had been given acclaim and roused controversy some ten years ago. I had been told, too often, that I really *ought* to read it and had once heard, more promisingly, 'it would be a marvellous film, but of course they can never make it'. A book which for any reason *cannot* be filmed sounds interesting.

William Golding starts with a very distinct situation, which any of his fellow novelists might envy him though it has been there for the taking long enough. An aeroplane crash-lands on an uninhabited coral island and the only survivors are a party of schoolboys. The author makes no fuss at all about contriving this, which shows his good sense, for if he had tried to make it more probable by supporting detail he might have shown up its near-impossibility, and it is unimportant anyway. In common with many thousand other readers I at once accepted from him that it had happened and was free to drive into the story.

But not before I had somewhat mischievously wondered what other writers would have made of that opening situation. I could guess fairly easily what Wells might have done with it for it was almost within his own scope. But what about Kipling? Or Buchan? Or Katherine Mansfield? There were writers who could not have tackled it at all, like D. H. Lawrence, and writers who might have turned it to something beautiful and macabre, like Walter de la Mare, or something vociferous and patchy, like M. P. Shiell. The imagination kicks at possible Russian versions or the mess that would be made of it by modern thriller writers of the Ian Fleming school.

[33]

The strength of William Golding's version, if one may call it so, is its inevitability. As one follows it one feels that he is right and repeats happily to oneself—'Yes. That's it. That's what would happen.' One cheers from the touchline right through.

For while tracing the all too credible events that follow the boy's landing, while appearing to do no more than give his reader a plain and factual account of how the children, individually and collectively, behaved, while never pausing to point morals or underline any recondite significances, Golding turns his little preparatory schoolboys and choristers in their school uniforms into naked savages, and shows the bloodlust and tyranny which break out as the inhibitions fall. He is satisfied with three deaths before the boys are rescued, but one of these, at least, is murder.

It sounds unbearably grim and nasty but it is saved by the character of one twelve-year-old, Ralph, who while remaining a perfectly natural boy, with nothing of the prig or storybook hero about him, keeps his sanity and, unconsciously, his inherent loyalties and decency, and not only saves the lives of the rest but saves the reader from nausea. For there also emerges the fascist dictator (Jack) who achieves his illicit leadership, after the election of Ralph, by offering to the mob the bread-and-circuses of roast pig and 'adventure', tribal dances and sadism, against poor Ralph's feeble democracy whose only ideal is to keep alive the smoke fire which may bring their rescue. The drawing of Ralph's character, only slightly exaggerated when he is too articulate in his speeches to the assembly, is sure and masterly and his story a truly moving one. Jack also is wholly credible unfortunately, for there had to be a Jack among so many human beings, though there might not have been a Ralph—a rarer phenomenon altogether.

It will be seen that for me at least this is one of those books one enters rather than reads. However improbable the initial set-up I was at once on the island with eyes and ears and emotions awake and had to be dragged away from it at the end. The story has true realism, the realism of *Alice in Wonderland*, *Wind in the Willows*, *Gulliver's Travels*, *Robinson Crusoe* and a score of other books which are based on factual improbabilities or impossibilities, but in which the authors have you eating out of their hands after a couple of pages.

This novel has other merits. The symbolism, if that is not too strong a word, is so artfully concealed that it never, like so much symbolism, becomes a bore. The brushwork is adequate but without virtuosity. The natural surroundings are there, accepted, and before the end of the book familiar, but never elaborately painted. And though the inferences are harsh if not tragic, and no concession is made to sentimentality, the final result is in some way comforting.

2

For most of the first day at sea the Spanish coast was on our port bow and it had an unfamiliar rather grim look. In summer the dry hills, like titanic brick-kilns, seem to bake and crackle in the sunlight, now snow-capped and misty they had a gaunt uninhabited look. When they at last had faded from view, the sea itself grew forbidding, a uniform dirty grey with unbroken sky-lines.

This, after all, was what I had come for, to escape the rich winter vegetation of Tangier and the petty comforts of my home and find the serenity of a shipboard routine. Though I had not expected to live in quite such isolation and silence, or to keep such monastically early hours, I found it all pleasant enough and soothing as the days began to pass.

[35]

After *Lord of the Flies* I wished I had more recent books and resolved if possible to correct this in Italian bookshops. Meanwhile I had a novel called *The Heat of the Day* by Elizabeth Bowen, an author taken seriously by her contemporaries. This was published first in 1949.

I met Elizabeth Bowen in what I imagine was her element. It certainly was not mine. I have never felt so miserably out of place and unwanted in my life. It was at a party given by Rose Macaulay in the Gargoyle in 1948 or 49, I think.

I had met Rose Macaulay herself only a few months earlier. I had collected her first editions since boyhood and when I asked her if she would inscribe them for me she said at once and with no affectation, gush or hauteur: 'Certainly. When would you like me to do it?' She had no patience with book-collecting, I think, but kind and downright she arranged to come to my flat and sign the lot.

She came in her traditionally frumpy clothes, driving across London in her old car. I once had to ride in that and it was a gruesome experience. A special fate must have watched over her as a driver. But she came, and sitting on my settee with a pile of her books beside her she signed them and piled them on the floor.

Over tea we discovered that we had both spent some time in Dernia, a small port in south-eastern Spain.

'I never thought anyone else knew it,' she said.

I said something about the shops there. 'I never look in shop windows abroad,' said Rose severely. A significant sentence. She was a little inhuman in such things.

Then she asked me to this party and without realizing what I was letting myself in for I accepted.

There they were, the literary upper ten, fearful lest they might become eleven, and watchful among the thirty or forty extras for anyone seeking a place in their counsels. At least so

it seemed to me who was very much an outsider. T. S. Eliot
wheeling John Hayward about in his invalid chair—but I
won't list the guests. I could do it on probability, even if I had
not been there. All those who 'never went to parties'. All who
had succeeded in creating a myth of remoteness. The only
likely figure missing was Charles Morgan, and he was dead.

I would have felt more depressed and inappropriate and
defiant if I had not come on Eddie Marsh whom I knew. He
must have guessed what I was going through for he took me
aside and talked till I could decently take my leave, treating me
as he had treated so many young men in his long dedicated life.
Not that I was young, in years, at any rate. I was not far short of
fifty, but among Rose's distinguished guests talking with a
deliberate lack of self-consciousness their esoteric shop, I felt
like a gauche adolescent and might have been one of the young
men whom Eddie Marsh had brought out thirty years before.

When I could, I fled. Then, in the lift, I found myself with
Elizabeth Bowen to whom I had been introduced half an hour
earlier. She was talking with Stephen Potter whom I knew by
sight but had always confused with a radio comedian of the
same surname.

What did I do? Break into their conversation? Wouldn't that
look as though I had deliberately timed my departure to talk
to Miss Bowen? She was book critic to the *Tatler* at the time
as I was to the *Sketch* and might think I wanted to comment on
the coincidence or even exchange impressions of that week's
books. On the other hand how could I say nothing? We had
just met and were now standing within a yard of one another
in that absurd metal-lined lift. To remain absolutely silent and
aloof would be, by my good middle-class standards, bearish
and rude.

But I need not have bothered. Miss Bowen gave me the
answer. She and her companion had entered the lift first and

[37]

stood at the back, pointedly face to face, pointedly in conversation. I closed the doors of the lift and glanced up, expecting at least a smile, or an indication of what was fairly obvious—that they wanted to stop at street level. No, they were talking heavily. I pressed the button and the lift ascended—for the party had been in a large room kept specially for such things in the basement. The lift stopped. Here was another quandary. Walk away, or let them pass? Either was feasible. In that small space and standing by the door I need not wait for 'ladies first', as my nurse had taught me. On the other hand I could not do that without at least turning to say good night. I decided to leave the initiative to Miss Bowen and stood back to allow her to pass. She did so, still talking to Stephen Potter, still without a nod or a smile.

Nervousness? Fear of an intruder? A natural inclination to snub strangers? A personal and deliberate thing done for some reason of which I knew nothing? Instinctive dislike or distrust of me? Genuine and complete absorption in a conversation of moment? I was amused and curious at the time but supposed I had long forgotten the incident.

I had, until I saw a photograph of Elizabeth Bowen heading the blurb of her novel *The Heat of the Day* and realized that I had never read a book of hers. Nor, incidentally, had I read a novel (and there must be several) set against the London blitz, as this was. Now I am wondering where its strength lies.

Not in its style, certainly. The ungainly stilt-walking prose, picking its way through a litter of unnecessary pronouns, prepositions and repetitions, seems to be attempting the precision of Henry James and becoming lost and tiresome in its faulty syntax. All those strings of little words which have to be read several times and then mean no more than a plain statement of half their combined length grow tedious after the first few pages. Not in the characterization, which is superficial and tittering, revealing snaps and twinkles of nature here and there, leaving no one whole or human. Not in the 'plot', which *is* a plot, sensational and obvious and based on a surprise, if not a surprise ending. The revelation that Robert is a spy and that Harrison really is a genuine security man is as much a trick development as anything in O. Henry. And not in the dialogue, which between the articulate characters is prosy and unnatural, but between Louie and Connie, the half-articulate, is laboured and false, as though the author had learnt pieces of idiom and characteristic turns of phrase from her daily char, and tried to insert them like discs of mirror in a Balkan embroidery.

Yet there is power in the book and immense readability. I swallowed it greedily, angered by every interruption. I forgot all its irritations and ended by liking it, as one comes to like a person one has thought unpleasant. Partly this was due to the author's restraint, which is much more than a negative virtue. She never appears to bother with her time and background, so enviably rich, the London of 1942 to 1945. Absorbed in her people she does not pause to paint a single scene. Yet it is vividly there and I, who never knew it, felt 'So *that's* what London was like when I was luckily abroad in the army'.

She is not afraid of ancient devices—like Ernestine's laugh and Harrison's double-taking eyes—yet she uses them so skilfully that one realizes only long afterwards that they are just those tricks of phrase by which Dickens distinguished one character from another. Moreover, though she does not make you feel for her characters or suffer with them, as Conrad can, she makes you recognize their feelings. 'I know just what she means,' you say, without surprise but with immense satisfaction. And though there is no switched-on humour in the book, no comedy contrived to lighten its shadows, you feel that the author is not lacking in humour and could write farce if she wished.

[39]

Yet that still does not answer the question and I remain at a loss to know why I liked a book of such obvious faults. I think perhaps it is that Elizabeth Bowen establishes her right to those faults since she has that rarest and best of qualities, a truly individual and original view of the world. She has, in simple terms, her own way of telling a story, of seeing, feeling and reporting on her fellow beings, in or out of crisis. Her tempo may be jumpy but it is her own. Her realism may be sketchy but because it is direct and unliterary and belongs to no one else, it is convincing. An exasperating author but certainly not one to ignore.

3

I went straight from *The Heat of the Day* to another book with a meteorological title, Louis Bromfield's *The Rains Came*. I had missed this when it was a best-seller twenty or thirty years ago. I expected it to be a little dated, but I knew it was still being read and discussed all over the world.

I came to it with a good deal of curiosity because it is about India. In fact it has probably given to several million Westerners their only inner vision of India, whether they have visited the sub-continent or not. That seems a lot of responsibility to heap on Bromfield's shoulders but I daresay they were broad enough to bear it.

As soon as I had read a chapter or two I realized that this was not any India I had known. This was a solidly created country with recognizable landmarks but it was not India of past or present. It might be India seen through the eyes of the *New Yorker*, or later, when Bromfield reaches absurdities like the interview between the Maharani and Aunt Phoebe, India seen through the eyes of David Harum. It was not a country but a backcloth and its characters did not live, but act.

A bit late and forlorn to come to these hasty conclusions about one of the most successful novels of the century, perhaps. I wondered what I should have thought if I had read it when it was first published in 1937 before I had seen something of India and while I still believed the experts could detect a fake. I should probably have been among its admirers. But not now. The quickness of the hand no longer deceives the eye.

Fascinated, I watched Bromfield brandish his facts and with a good deal of virtuosity introduce his knowledge, zoological, botanical, geographical, meteorological and all the rest. I knew instinctively that he would not make a single slip here, that the book had been written after scrupulous research and later fine-tooth-combed by experts for anything that could be called an error.

Yet the whole damned thing is a lie and every character in the book, Hindu, Muslim, English, American, Scottish and Eurasian is a Middle Westerner in a meticulously correct disguise. One is conscious almost immediately, in the first few chapters, that the author lives in fear of this, is firmly determined that it shall not be so and puts up a game fight, with every scrap of local colour he can muster to help him, to avoid it. His noises, his scents, his faces, his costumes, his trees, his birds, his architecture—he uses them all, artfully and aptly. But he can't change the people to whom he gives likely, well-thought-out names. They are all from Ohio, brown or white, old or young.

Not all his effort is wasted, however. He does give the reader that essential curiosity about what is going to happen. This is a test for both the reader and the storyteller, I think. It does not matter, on a certain level, that the world created is a false one with hybrid impossible inhabitants, if the author can persuade

[41]

the reader to accept it and be interested in what goes on in it. This, to some extent, Bromfield does. Even after my three years in India which prejudice me from the start against most European attempts to interpret it, which make me prefer a scrap of a short story by Narayan to the whole of *A Passage to India* or *Hindu Holiday*, even after those years, I did want to know what would happen in Bromfield's state of Ranchipur and, though with an effort and reservations, accepted its existence, persuaded by Bromfield's narrative energy and evident good will.

I accepted it, that is, until things began to happen, cataclysmic things like flood and fire and pestilence. These showed, alas, the basic unreality of the creatures I was watching, showed them to be of ink and paper and clever cerebral mist, not of flesh and blood. For the very flood is not an inevitable force of nature, like Conrad's *Typhoon*, it is a super cinematic effect created without any thought of expense by a brilliant producer. It is inevitable only in that it was pre-planned, minutely and authentically, but none the less in a writer's brain, not on the ground. And as the characters begin to react to it one sees that they too had been created for this very purpose, to behave with awful literary unexpectedness in the circumstances. One is angry because one has gone along with Bromfield, liked him as he laboured away, appreciated many of his touches, smiled with him in his moments of humour and joined him in his small triumphs of research and psychology. One feels let down.

In some of the last chapters, the book degenerates into mush and folksiness which are unforgivable. This is not so much in the love scenes which are like most post-Hemingway love scenes, but in other less palatable moments. In Smiley, Bromfield was evidently trying to create a good man who is not a bore and succeeded only in pulling a rabbit out of his hat. In the Maharani he sought to personify that corny conception, the wise old woman of the East. He produced a coffee-coloured Eleanor Roosevelt. And so on. It is not easy to finish the book when the flood has gone down, because—and this is the real measure of the author's failure—one does not care who has gone with it. If this kind of fiction can't make one care, what can it do?

How much better it would have been, I thought ungratefully, if instead of trying to interpret an existing foreign country to his own compatriots, Bromfield had created one for himself. How much easier, too.

I had with me a novel by an author, Patrick Leigh Fermor, who did just that. It was called *The Violins of Saint-Jacques* and it was, according to reviews quoted on the back of it, 'a beautiful little tour-de-force' (Betjeman) and 'a perfectly successful small masterpiece'. Both terms are apt to be used too freely and I began to read with the greatest suspicion.

This was by no means dissipated when I found it took the form of imaginary reminiscences, a story supposed to be told by a wise old Lesbian living in Mitylene, a sort of female Marlow. This was a method which might, of course, produce a 'masterpiece' but was not reassuring to a Conradian like me. I could listen to Marlow all night, as his hearers often did, because he did so much more than tell a story. But what would Berthe de Rennes with her 'intelligent, hawkish and most distinguished face' have to offer which the author could not tell me himself?

There was another irritation. The Penguin blurb speaks of 'the beginning of the last century' as the time of events in the book, whereas they take place at the beginning of this one.

One way or another I was put off the book and though I knew of Patrick Leigh Fermor that he was an intimate of many of my friends ('Haven't you met Paddy Lee Fermor? I wonder why not') and though I was predisposed towards a book about

D

a vanished island, I admitted that had I still been reviewing this might have gone into *Books in Brief* with an impatient three-line notice written on the strength of the blurb. That would have been a mistake.

For Patrick Leigh Fermor has one quite extraordinary gift, among, but dwarfing, many others. I can find no word for it—it is not imagination exactly, or realism, or a talent for description or evocation, but perhaps a combination of these. I can best show what I mean by naming a few books which display it most happily, Thornton Wilder's *The Bridge of San Luis Rey*, Conrad's *Nostromo*, Richard Hughes's *A High Wind in Jamaica*, Prokosch's *The Asiatics*, Maurice Hewlett's *Little Novels of Italy*. It consists in taking a place and a period just far enough out of sight to escape a tiresome factuality and with a little research, avoidance of crude anachronisms or annoying improbabilities, moulding it nearer to the heart's desire. More than that, telling a story of people made all the more real because their behaviour cannot be criticized or doubted from the reader's experience, in a setting which becomes vivid by its very exoticism. Done well, this leads to rich results. Done badly, to another tatty costume romance asking for Hollywood treatment.

Fermor does it well. His island—which disappeared into the sea after an eruption of its volcano fifty years ago—is more vivid to us than it could have been to its most observant visitor. His people breathe and have their period being. Although his climax was ready made, as it were, the climax of Lytton's *Last Days of Pompeii*, he brings us to it with such persuasive detachment that we watch it as an event at which we might have been spectators. Fermor sheds no crocodile tears and wastes no sentiment. He records, and in such detail that he might indeed have been recalling, as his Berthe de Rennes is supposed to be doing. But for a tendency to show off the results of his research by descriptive lists of trivia, his telling of the story is faultless and assured. It is a book to enjoy—and there's the rub.

Should it be a book to enjoy, the story of a disaster which wiped out forty thousand people, a score of whom had become known to the reader? Is there not something missing in such a book, that one remains quite unmoved as the last of the red-hot island sinks into the sea? Should one be delighting in the brilliant prose in which all this is written? But one is. Masterly, one says, reading the unhurried terrible lines recording the destruction. Masterly—but a masterpiece? Not quite, for Fermor has chosen to paint a vast tragedy as an exquisite miniature. Betjeman was right. It is a *tour de force*.

But one not to be missed. A book like this, standing up among all the rubble and slag of contemporary fiction like an architect's dream, white and brilliant against the grime of industrialism, is something to remember. Or better to forget, so that one can return to it in a few years' time as one returns to a favourite landscape.

4

SAVONA

In the early afternoon of Friday, that is just a week after I had left Tangier, the coast of Italy became visible and soon I could distinguish the buildings of Savona round the bay we were approaching.

Would I have recognized the landscape as Italian if I had not known where the ship lay, or have seen it merely as an unspecified Mediterranean coastline? The mountains above the town were slate blue but behind them were mistier mountains fading into a frowning sky. They could be Spanish, I supposed, and so perhaps could be the architecture. Yet I fancied there was something here more fresh and clean-cut, more trim perhaps. No ancient buildings could be picked out as we approached but ugly green tenement blocks and the idiot façades of modern buildings on a dozen floors, smirking in the pale January sunlight.

I was impatient to go ashore, however, for it was twenty-three years since I had been in Italy and here, I thought, in this busy little port, after Genoa and Nice the most important city of the Riviera, I should have my first sight of post-war Italy.

We anchored a mile or so from the shore and a launch came out with officials of the Port Authority but there was no bustle on board as on a ship coming to port and I questioned the Chief Steward who was my only contact with the bridge. His English was scanty and he spoke no French or Spanish but I managed to extricate a few facts. The port was congested after delays caused by the recent storms and there were twenty-three ships waiting to go in. We were expected to stay out here three days but in the morning the Captain was going ashore on a launch and would take me if I wished. We had cargo for three days' unloading so it looked as though we should be here for the best part of a week.

There was nothing to do but be patient but I felt some exasperation that evening when at the absurd hour of six-thirty the Chief Steward proudly produced as the first course of dinner a dish of fresh, or at least deep-frozen, asparagus which had been fried in butter and sprinkled with fried breadcrumbs, grated cheese and drops of bottled tomato ketchup. Boris, watching for a chance to light my cigar or hand me an ashtray, informed me that his cigarettes were running out again as he had owed so many to the crew. Savona and the prospect of Italy had become a string of lights round the bay and an icy north wind came down on us from the Alps if not the Arctic. It was not in the best of humours, therefore, that I picked up *Mr Nicholas* by Thomas Hinde.

2

When I was an opinionated young man, passionately discussing contemporary novelists and confidently deciding whether Wells or Lawrence would 'live', I thought of books not as 'good' or 'bad' but as 'great' or 'negligible' and was irritated by those which escaped both categories, not being written by morons for morons on the one hand or being absolutely certain of immortality on the other. I had no place for the merely readable, the convincing, suspenseful books which I had for years enjoyed.

Where, I wonder, would I have put Thomas Hinde's *Mr Nicholas*? It is not perhaps a 'great' novel but it is certainly not a negligible one. Indeed I am inclined to think that if the author had been less a student of Freud and more of Dostoievski, say; less of a psychiatrist and more of a novelist, I would have plumped, even in those exigent days, for the highest category. It is certainly a remarkable book in a number of unexpected ways.

Thomas Hinde, although this was a first novel when it appeared in 1952, has the unusual ability to set his own tempo and gear his reader down to it. He moves on unconcerned among the familiar trivialities of upper middle class suburban life in a house of french windows and a tennis court, as though he had never seen a play by A. A. Milne. He is not worried lest his reader, after a dozen pages, should yawn and say: What, again?' He knows he has a story to tell and there is only one way to tell it, quietly and mercilessly, never neglecting a point, never skimping a scene, never blurring a detail.

And the reader is soon rewarded. The atmosphere may be familiar but Hinde lights it with such skill that it is intensified like a brightly illumined stage. Not that there is anything in the least stagey about the dialogue, or cinematographical about the setting. Both are cruelly commonplace. But the author makes one notice things, throws a light on this object or that, points out an idiosyncrasy, makes audible an undertone. He is determined that one should miss nothing and he is uncannily successful.

When I had got the measure of Mr Nicholas the man (as I thought) I began to enjoy myself immensely. I had never met this particular paterfamilias in a novel before, but gosh, how well I knew him in life! Gently and with explicit reason dominating his wife and sons, complacently aware of the excellence of his own motives, believing absolutely in himself, he must bring a shudder to all the generation whose fathers fought in the First World War. Couldn't I hear his 'You see, old chap. . .' and his 'Just as you think, my dear, but . . .' and his genial 'Did you hear about my row with the committee?' He is an everyday monster, a grinding bore, an egomaniac whose ravings we have taken for granted all our lives.

We are under a spell, no less, as we watch this appalling family in its everyday life. We are mesmerized as we recognize in it so much of all family life, heightened by a hidden intensity. The incidents are not seen but remembered from long-ago observation. The people are not characters but ourselves and our neighbours, a shade distorted for the author's purpose but acutely recognizable. Intimacies, conversations, petty dramas, incidents, it continues relentlessly till we are almost crying for relief.

But relief when it comes is disappointment, too. We grow aware that the author has his plans for a climax and with its explosion will wreck the whole beautiful symmetry of his work. For he would have us believe that Mr Nicholas, that gruesome mediocrity, that exemplar of his time and class and background, is not the fabulous but familiar beast we supposed him, but a madman, a stark certifiable lunatic who at the end of the book is on his way to confinement.

I reject this with the indignation of a hitherto more than interested reader. If Mr Nicholas is mad so are two-thirds of a generation. If the textbook symptoms which appear in the last pages were latent in his character all the time, not

[49]

only have his wife and sons been deceived but the reader as well.

Thomas Hinde is obviously not a writer to concoct the final melodrama merely as an effective climax. He must believe in the mental breakdown of Mr Nicholas. I see now that he has laid a few clues to this development in the body of the book, as when Mr Nicholas hears an unaccountable buzzing noise. But they were so irrelevant to the text that I had not noticed them. I see, too, that Mr Nicholas *might* go mad as anyone might, but that is not what I am meant to conclude. His madness is intended to be a natural development from his character and that I cannot, dare not, believe. I think the author has let himself be guided by the propositions of psychology instead of the laws of dramatic truth.

That seems common enough in modern fiction. Plenty of novels have been made from a couple of pages of Freud, but not novels as good as this. It is putting the cart before the horse, surely. The psychologist should be able to learn from the novelist; the novelist will never learn anything from the cut-and-dried theories of the psychologist.

I would like to dismiss the book's ending as an unfortunate afterthought, but I am told it was intended from the beginning. Hinde was depicting a paranoid psychotic, we learn from the blurb. It is, I think, a tribute to him that we cannot accept this. He was depicting a middle-class middle-aged Englishman of some intelligence, a fearsome egotist who could see no one's point of view but his own and covered this disability with a bluff of reasonableness, a man not wholly without charm and his own kind of integrity who, above all, was always, secretly or openly, in the right. He was depicting all our fathers, and I for one cannot believe that all our fathers were paranoid psychotics who ended, or should have ended, by being certified. But how superbly well he *is* depicting them, and their families,

[50]

homes and friends, their wives and their interests. At times the verisimilitude is unbearable.

Moreover if I try to think how else he could have brought his book to a close I am at a loss. Perhaps by making the crisis one for only the younger generation—though that's an old gambit. Perhaps by having no crisis at all but leaving that unhappy family to continue, as it does continue around us everywhere. But that might be too near the knuckle. Perhaps with a murder, but that would be asking for misunderstanding. Yet anything, for me, would have been better than this piece of routine psychiatry at the end of a story which has broken with so many routines.

3

I was becoming accustomed to the ship's timetable and it did not seem bizarre next morning to find myself bathed, shaved, breakfasted and ready to go ashore before eight o'clock. A launch came alongside but the sea was rough enough to make boarding her a perilous piece of timing and agility. An old boatman helped me aboard and shouted to me not to stay in the bows of the launch because I should get wet. For some reason I ignored this advice and was lucky to get only a light dash of spray on the way across.

The port was jammed with shipping from both sides of the Curtain. There was a U.S. destroyer lying against the quay, manned apparently by lounging slobs who, hands in pockets, gaped longingly at 'Ma's Place', a café started for their benefit across the road.

We landed by the Torre Leon Pancaldo, an ancient tower which stands alone overlooking the docks. The city's emblem,

[51]

and known familiarly as the Torretta, it was probably a part of the first city wall and built before the eleventh century. It has a notable statue of Our Lady of Pity with the inscription *In mare irato, in subita procella, invoco te, nostra benigna Stella.* Standing there backed by modern buildings with noisy traffic round its base the tower is like a squat rough parody of Venice's graceful *campanile*.

From it I crossed to the central thoroughfare of the town which runs directly inland, the Via Paleocapa. This is a fine street, wide and arcaded.

But the town was scarcely awake and the air was ferociously cold. I walked under the arcades for the length of the street finding all the shops shut and only an occasional citizen, wrapped up to the ears, hurrying by. I returned by the arcade on the other side of the street and found the first shop to open was a barber's and in competition there were soon other barbers at work under bright electric light in the chilly half darkness of morning. There seemed to be at least a dozen barbers' shops in the street for Italy is one of the few countries where men still like to be shaved.

Slowly the city came to life. Cafés were the next to open, then one after another the shops. The wide pavements under the arcades meanwhile had grown populous with office workers, shop-assistants and early shoppers, hurrying, warmly dressed folk who chattered, not like the idling crowds of noon in summer, but chattering sharply as they walked or worked.

I forgot the cold in a mood of happy response to this awakening. After years of muezzin whines it was glorious to hear the tinny impatient church bells. After *jelabbas* and sandals it was good to see the neat little housewives' twinkling stiletto heels. The smell of coffee was strong, the colours came out in shop windows artificially lit, schoolchildren gabbled by and everything was brisk and purposeful.

That was it. A crowded street in North Africa seems to lack all purpose. Standing, sauntering, arguing, squatting, the people are there like figures in a canvas. Some of them may be passing through on some errand but for most of them to be there is sufficient. This is attractive to watch and reassuring to those who think that too much purpose and haste lead to destruction. But to live within perpetual sight of it, as I do, gives a return to the north a peculiar delight. These are one's own people leading lives one understands. In London, Cologne, Zurich or here in Savona the early-morning tempo is about the same, whereas in the south or east it is a yawning, scratching, sleepy-eyed thing.

Otherwise, how could I have taken such pleasure in watching that not very interesting city going about the business of a January day?

4

I went into a café and ordered coffee and brandy. The coffee was a mouthful in a minute cup, the brandy was raw Italian grape spirit very welcome in that icy morning air. I watched the customers coming in quickly, standing at the counter to swallow their little gulps of *espresso* and hurrying out again. Alone or in groups they came and gave themselves scarcely time to greet the proprietor, drink their coffee and take their leave. Strange, this, if not unique. In France, in Spain, even in England coffee in the morning seems a mere excuse for conversation; in Italy they drink it for itself. Or it is a nervous habit, like cigarette-smoking? I remained, alone in a comfortable chair, while a changing stream of imbibers flowed past.

The proprietor came and talked to me, his manner very

[53]

different from the traditionally over-courteous one of innkeepers and barmen in novels about Italy. Those smiling, bowing
men, their speech full of '*Signore*' and '*Molta grazzie*', with
their servile obeisances must have gone with pre-war Italy to
Hollywood. This man was not impolite, but direct and a little
familiar. 'How old are you?' I remember him asking, to follow
the question with his own age. Was I off a ship? Was I a ship's
officer? I was pleased to find that Italian, unspoken these twenty
years, came back to me, and though I mixed it with some
Spanish rather than hesitate, it was comprehensible to my
questioner.

I had some shopping to do. I had left my razor behind and
had been using Boris's. What the hell was a razor in Italian?
I tried a farmacia but when the assistant gathered what I meant
by an '*aparato por far la barba*' he sent me to a *profumeria*. One
is as logical as the other, I suppose; in England or Italy why do
we buy razors at chemists? A large bookshop at the top of the
street had a fine show of Penguins and I laid out a few pounds
on them, delighted to find on an obscure shelf an Italian translation of a book of mine *Nove Giorni con Edoardo*. Then to
change some money and buy some cigars.

I had an hour to pass before the launch would leave for the
the *Trepča* and found myself returning to the same café. How
quickly and easily we form habits. A chair in a neighbour's
house once sat in is chosen automatically on return. One pub in
a village out of several, one brand of cigarettes, one route from
place to place, one trick of speech adopted unwarily, each
becomes one's own and the devil cannot shift it from favour. I
returned to this café without thinking, because I had been there
before. It remained 'my' café all the time we were in Savona.

Down at the docks, awaiting the launch, my attention was
caught by an old character in a pea-jacket. He was of the sea
unmistakably, and more, of the Mediterranean sea. A nobbly

weather-beaten face, bright restless eyes, brisk movements and broad gestures, he moved among the men on the waterfront, talking with a hurried grin that disappeared almost before it had come, gesticulating with ferocity, shouting, enjoying himself, a Conrad character, jumpy as a marionette. An artist might have wanted to sketch him, as I did in the clumsier medium of words.

Then a car drew up and a young man, from an office in the city I judged, made towards the old sailor I had been watching. The sailor's hands went deep into the pockets of his pea-jacket and he ostentatiously looked out to sea. The young man talked for a minute to be answered by a heavy shrug of the shoulders and no more. He pulled out some papers but though the old eyes flickered round for a moment the pea-jacket hung still, like a coat on a statue.

Suddenly the sailor turned. His hands came out of his pockets and began their violent motions. He spoke with such emphasis that his eyes grew angry and his voice a shout. He spoke at length. The young man seemed to expect this and remained calm. Then, the storm over, the sailor was once more motionless and staring out to sea.

It went on. There was another exchange after which the young man produced money, but apparently not enough for it brought nothing but an absent shake of the head from the sailor, who had again returned to horizon watching. A third party was appealed to without success. An office window near by was visited briefly but those behind it were unable to help. A new outburst from the sailor, who raised his arms high in despair, wagged his finger in warning, stamped his foot in exasperation and shouted in apparent fury, was followed by yet another period of stillness and inscrutability. To this the young man responded by a calm proposition spoken into a seemingly inattentive hairy ear. The effect was slow but defini-

[55]

tive. No eager agreement was voiçed but a hand came out of the jacket pocket and took a number of lira notes, returning to the depths again. There was a long pause before hurried smiles broke, goodbyes were said and the young man returned to his car. Throughout the scene no one except me had paid the slightest attention to it.

5

I decided not to go ashore again by launch but to wait till the *Trepča* was in harbour. Time enough then to see the town and no limit to my hours ashore, as today when I kept a rendezvous to return to the ship.

Instead I examined my new Penguins and decided on one called *A Rose by Any Other Name* by Anthony Carson. It did not occur to me that this could be a pen-name chosen by an author in preference to his own, indeed I felt some sympathy with a man branded with this novelettish name and wondered whether the book's title referred wistfully to his fate. Carson, Carstairs, Cardew, Carruthers, Cardigan, Cartright, Carmarthen, Cartland, Carberry, Carew, Carleton, Carmichael—surely every serial-story-writer had had her pick at these?

But when I opened the book and looked at the author's portrait I saw it was a man I had known as Peter Brooke. Moreover there was an assurance from Colin MacInnes that Anthony Carson was 'one of the few great humorous writers of the century'. Even allowing for the flighty enthusiasms and acerbities of reviewers, with both of which I was familiar, this was incredible, for the thing Peter Brooke had lacked most was any of that blessed and essential humour which shows a man that he himself is funny. He was not without wit at the expense of others but he was far too earnest a person, with far too serious objects in life, to give himself any scope for laughter.

I used to meet him at a pub called the Wheatsheaf in the 1940s. Solemn, dedicated and ponderous, he hungered after two things—publication and food.

'I must find a publisher for My Novel,' he used to say rather menacingly. His hunger for food was not caused by poverty but by a superb capacity for large meals. Perhaps the two hungers were in some way connected.

'What kind of novel is it?' someone asked.

'It's based on my own experience,' said Peter Brooke severely.

He talked of 'experience' as though it were a commodity in which he had invested, of which he now held a large stock ready to be put on the market.

'What kind of experience?' persisted his questioner.

Mostly his experience as a courier to a travel agency, it appeared, but there were other things. He had a lot of experience.

Nearly everyone who came to the Wheatsheaf in those days had an inkling that he himself and the rest of us were somewhat laughable figures, even Julian Maclaren-Ross who wore a disintegrating teddy-bear coat, carried an ornate walking-stick and bagged the corner place at the bar so that he could lecture the rest of us from a vantage point. Even one of Freud's grandsons—not the painter but a young man in publishing. Even Dylan Thomas, drunk or sober. Even the young men who did unrecognizable sketches of the customers at half a crown a time. But not Peter Brooke. He could see nothing funny in himself, or in not being able to get his work published when it was so full of experience, and nothing at all funny in having a perpetually unassuaged appetite.

Somebody must once have told him that his eyes were

[57]

mesmeric for he had a trick of opening them very wide at you and trying to stare you out. 'This novel of mine . . .' he would say, bringing the conversation back to the point at which he had left it.

I volunteered to read the novel at last, for at the Wheatsheaf we were all a little tired of it. I found it sound solid stuff about a heroic courier to a travel agency and the situations he came up against. Whatever was funny in the book it was not the travel agent's courier. He was a mesmeric man, brimming with experience, not at all a man to laugh at.

It seemed just the book for the literary agent who acted for me then and I introduced Peter Brooke to him. I was not mistaken. It was promptly placed with one of the Hutchinson companies. But it did not sell and Peter Brooke's manner to me grew rather reproachful afterwards. His stock of experience had been expended in vain.

I saw him once more, still Peter Brooke, still profoundly concerned with himself, still hungry, in Tangier. He was, of course, living in the Medina, where all really serious-minded artists and local-colour-seekers are to be found. He had given up novel-writing, he said, and was working on a play with a Canadian happily named Wanklyn. They shared an incredibly Moorish house in a dark Moorish alley and they were full of purpose. Peter Brooke was putting his experience into the play and Christopher Wanklyn was a good cook. They took a night off to come and eat curry in my house and at the sight of its first dish on the table Peter Brooke said: 'I can't possibly wait for the rest of this—*I must start*,' and did so. He ate himself into a boa-constrictor's coma and for the first time in my memory he smiled and ceased to talk about his experience or his work.

So now he was Anthony Carson, 'one of the few great English humorous writers of the century'. Moreover he contributed, said the blurb, to both the *New Statesman* and *Punch*.

[*58*]

I rarely see these periodicals but from what I remembered of them it was something of a feat to be a Highest Common Factor, or even a Lowest Common Multiple, to the two. What was this extraordinary metamorphosis? I could not wait, as they say, to read the book.

It was funny. No doubt of that. Not uproariously or too subtly, yet honestly laughter-provoking. But what was most interesting was the theme, the *line*, of all its humour. The travel agent's courier had ceased to be upstanding and heroic and become a Mr Pooter, dogged by misadventure, the butt of circumstances, lamentable and absurd. In delightfully casual little sketches he travels several continents, pitiful, laughable, irresistible. Gone are the mesmeric eyes and gone, one feels, is the hunger. Here is a happy buffoon.

What had happened? It was quite simple, really. The penny had dropped. Anthony Carson had seen the joke and Peter Brooke was the cream of it.

6

I came to know Savona in the five days that followed as one knows a town one has chosen for a long holiday. I had been right that first morning—the arcaded street running from the docks to the Piazza del Popolo and the station was more than the backbone of the town, it was almost the town itself and no shops of importance were out of it. 'Piazza del Popolo', to what series of heroes had that little square of garden been dedicated, I wondered, before it had been offered to The People? Garibaldi's myriad monuments for the most part survived Mussolini and Piazza Garibaldi was common enough, but there must have been some street signs and inscriptions on marble to

E

change, some maps and atlases to alter, some statuary to remove when Mussolini fell. We are fortunate in England in never having taken to changing our street names with our governments and sticking to Cromwell Road and Victoria Station, Wellington or Marlborough Street. We seem to be fairly wary in giving names, however, choosing for the most part heroes of the far past beyond controversy, or nonentities of more recent years, rather than committing ourselves in a moment of national enthusiasm to something that would *have* to be changed when sobriety returned, like Lloyd George Avenue. The Italians have never shown this restraint so that municipalities must have to work hard in keeping their street-names up to date. Piazza del Popolo sounds a fairly safe one, at least for the present.

It was not very impressive, Savona. A pleasant busy town of pleasant busy people. I was happy in it because it was Italy after Morocco, because it was Christian and European, because I had time to know it and like it, but I had to admit that there was nothing startling to see or exciting to do.

There was one of those pretentious civic theatres which seem to have been erected all over Italy in the last century. It was named after Savona's most famous son, the poet Gabriello Chiabrera.

I had always felt some curiosity about this sixteenth-century character, a contemporary of Shakespeare and Cervantes who believed he was changing the world's literary history by his massive epics, pastorals and satires and who lives now by a few *canzonetti* and *scherzi* written to be set to music. His picture of himself as an old man is endearing, too. He had a simple-hearted, passionate adoration of all things Greek and 'good as Greek poetry' was his yardstick of excellence. He loved journeys and sight-seeing, detested literary conversation, and relived his hours of triumph when favours were shown him by princes

[*60*]

and the Pope. He was a little vain and vengeful but was a quiet Christian to his death. He spoke of his *infinita maraviglia* of Virgil and loved masculine rhymes and blank verse, a crusty, likeable probably rather garrulous old man who had returned to his native town to live, and die in his eighty-seventh year.

The history of Savona seems to have been a long struggle to exist as a port only twenty odd miles from Genoa. In the twelfth century the Savonese had already built themselves a harbour but in the sixteenth the Genoese rendered it useless by sinking stone-filled ships in its mouth, on the pretext that the French might use it for trade or attack. The Genoese also destroyed Savona's oldest cathedral and the present one, a late Renaissance building, was started in 1589 and has a Baroque façade not built till 1886. Inter-city strife was as much a part of ancient Italy as inter-league football is of modern England.

7

Each day in Savona was for me minutely eventful. There was the day we were taken in by tugs and tied up to the end of the jetty, not yet alongside, not yet able to discharge cargo, but presumably next in the queue. To go ashore meant being taken by rowing boat to slippery stone steps and walking half a mile through the docks, dodging lorries and cranes.

The Russian crew of a cargo boat lying only a few yards from us showed not the smallest awareness of our presence, though some Finns on the other side shouted as we came in. The Russian ship had a noticeably trim and polished look and its sailors, like all sailors, were cheerful. They were recognizable as Slavs, but no more. I should have known they were not Germans, Scandinavians or Latins but found them indistinguishable from other Slavs. This was the first time I had seen the Hammer and Sickle flying from a masthead.

The next day broke gloriously with sunlight on the snow caps of the mountains and on the decks of ships about us, a cold, sparkling merry morning which made me hurry in to town to be greeted as an old customer in my little café.

The next, as the sunlight persisted, I took a taxi out to Albisola, a seaside town a mile or two away. Highly coloured and cheerful, with the sea breaking only a few yards from the cafés and hotels along the beachside road, it was unmistakably an empty summer resort. Beach furniture was lashed in piles and it was hard not to populate the sands with sunburnt crowds.

I lunched at a clean sunny restaurant and ate *ravioli* and sole. They had served some *pasta* dishes on board, the usual soggy parodies of the real thing, which should be made fresh every day and actually is in millions of Italian kitchens. *Ravioli* are an elaboration, probably only a century or two old, but the *pasta* in one form or another has been eaten here since Roman times and no more loses its place in Italian diet than rice does in Indian.

My sole was brought for my inspection uncooked on a trolley with a large assortment of sea monsters of many shapes, including wicked little *calamares* and ferocious scampi. It appeared later superbly cooked but I was rash enough to drink an Italian white wine with it. Will I never learn that my stomach is a snob and contemptuously rejects all small wines, all *ordinaires*, all Algerian, Moroccan, Yugoslav, South African, Australian, Californian wine, indeed everything but fine claret and burgundy, hock, a few Rhone wines, champagne and the fortified wines of Spain, Portugal and Madeira? I was not brought up like a Frenchman on sound table wine at every meal, believing that all wine is good, though some better than others. In my childhood—and all our tastes and habits in food and drink

[62]

derive from childhood—I was given wine seldom but what I drank was exceptionally good. Hence my lack of a good catholic taste in wine now. That Orvieto was a mistake.

As yet unwarned of this I ordered cheese with which to finish the bottle and was thinking how good it was to get a real Bel Paese instead of the phony imitations sold out of Italy, when two men came in and took the table next to mine. I gathered they lived on some kind of sailing craft. One was a bearded American, lean, ginger-haired and foxy, the other an Englishman, tanned, solid, with rimless glasses looking out of place on his square-set face. The American was garrulous, the Englishman had an air of reserve and sagacity. The more the American rattled on, informing, questioning, almost pleading, the more judicial became the Englishman's manner. I knew, as one instinctively knows things about one's own compatriots, that behind that façade of profundity and sapience the Englishman had a dull conventional mind, but the American did not know this and talked liberally as though egged on by his friend's 'Yes. I should think so', 'I'd say undoubtedly', 'Possibly, but isn't that rather an assumption?' and so on.

With the fish the American grew positively feverish in his appeals until I longed to tell him to give it up. 'There's nothing *there*,' I wanted to say. 'You're throwing yourself against a brick wall'—an apt and pleasing metaphor. Perhaps the Orvieto was already turning sour.

I left them and strolled along the esplanade, looking up to the snow-capped hills sparkling under the sun or out to sea where still more ships awaited entry to Savona harbour. I saw a little baroque church a few yards uphill from the beach and visiting it found the interior one nightmare of gold leaf and murals. Not nightmare, perhaps; in a more placid mood I might have responded to the rococo shell, so lavish, so opulent. But not that day, and when I saw scaffolding and realized that two

[63]

workmen were regilding a duller patch or two, I crossed myself at the stoup and left precipitately.

8

While the *Trepča* was in dock there seemed to be an air of relaxation, even gaiety, among the crew and that evening some of them were singing in the saloon with banjo accompaniment. My cabin was next door and when I went to bed they stopped abruptly. I was growing rather tired of this excessive politeness and disciplined reserve on board but it certainly gave me the solitude I wanted.

When at last we left Savona it was in a driving snowstorm.

5

GENOA

We reached Genoa in two hours but again had to lie outside because of congested shipping in the port. During the journey and the day's waiting which followed I read a book by a more popular novelist, Vicki Baum. It was her last novel and was called *Ballerina*.

Somebody, I hope, will write a biography of Vicki Baum, who died in 1960. A great deal has been lost in England by our failure in this century to encourage biographers to undertake the lives of minor writers of merit and so follow the interplay of literary life. Perhaps commercially many of them do not justify the undertaking but it seems a pity that they should be left to a time when all their contemporaries are dead and their bones must be picked by strangers. I can at once think of half a dozen whose lives might produce truly interesting books which, so far as I know, have yet to be written—J. D. Beresford, Leonard Merrick, May Sinclair, W. B. Maxwell, Dorothy Richardson, W. L. George. These were, roughly speaking, contemporaries and their lives had points of contact, so that if they are neglected some lively material will go *en masse* to oblivion.

Vicki Baum was of a later generation and a very different tradition. Her work in conception was more ambitious than any of these and perhaps in achievement less, but she has a place of a sort in this century's letters and deserves commemoration.

What a magnificent old pro of a writer she was! How minutely she drew up a small-scale map of the territory she was going to enter, how studiously covered every detail of research. Then—or so it appears from her books—when she had learned the language like a native, met everyone worth meeting, prepared her camping kit to the last mosquito net, she was off on her safari after rare characters and hairbreadth escapes from the big bad wolf of banality, and at last a few fine bits of taxidermy for the halls of her fame.

Where does this fall down? Why are her books no more than good stories told with supreme competence? To say that she had talent but no genius is not enough. Writers of genius have written worse and writers of far less talent have achieved better moments, at least. To say that to succeed on the scale she planned would have needed a Titan may be nearer the truth, for she certainly aimed high. I think the only explanation that satisfies me requires a new metaphor. She tried to run up with ferro-concrete what the old cathedral builders created over several centuries with carved stone, imagination, faith and love. So her novels are all glinting new, constructed on the latest plan by the most modern method and have, ultimately, nothing in them.

Ballerina is an able piece of work if ever there was one. I do not know whether someone who has given a lifetime to dancing would recognize it as the truth about that eerie and unnatural profession—I know I do. Or at least *a* truth. As feat and outwardly effortless, as artificial and faultless as ballet itself, it holds

[66]

something more than one's attention, as good ballet always does. And yet . . .

The last climax, anyway, is vulgar and conventional. The quite unbelievable attempt of the prima ballerina's doctor husband to make something of an affair with a hoydenish young girl and to drop it like a hot brick at Katja's summons makes a nice neat happy ending suitable for a two-hour film but is an insult to the reader who has paid Vicki Baum the compliment of believing in her people and watching with interest their movements and motives. Perhaps it represents the triumph of the scenario-writer in Vicki Baum. In 1931 she went to America and, says the blurb of *Ballerina*, 'fell in love with the country'. She lived in Hollywood. Perhaps she learned to twist her stories to the purposes of the screen, knowingly depriving her characters of that inevitability in their behaviour which should have been their carat stamp.

That is the effect, anyway. The reader is ultimately let down. But it says much for Vicki Baum's gift of realism that the reader minds so much.

2

Genoa from the sea is a modern city. As one stares at the apartment and office blocks, some of them twenty storeys high, one knows that among them must be fine old streets and ancient buildings but all is obliterated by this cubist foreground, this pattern of child's bricks in pastel colours. Yet the whole landscape, in its entirety, is superb, for this city was built on so narrow a level at the mountain's foot that it has had to climb and one sees its suburbs breaking into scattered villages, and these in turn to isolated villas high towards the snowy hilltops.

[67

I looked at those villages from the deck of the *Trepča* and remembering all village life round the Mediterranean, which I had seen north and south, I thought what pretty sentimental pieces I could write about them after a few months in one of them—the village priest, the mayor, the intrusive pigs, the daughter of the innkeeper, that sort of thing. But I never should spend months, or even days, on the hills above Genoa, for life there would be insanitary, uncomfortable and crude and I was no longer a youth to want to enter every promising landscape seen from the sea. Besides, it is corny just now, that rustic half-humorous half-nostalgic writing, especially when it is placed in Italy.

No. If a modern writer wanted to use any of this scene as a background, he would have to stay down in the docks among the tenement houses and general ugliness, the violent heroic characters of the dock-workers, the struggles of the union leaders, the bare hard conditions of life where television was still a luxury. He would keep his eyes off those hillsides, forget that cosy little vendetta that started when a farmer lost his cow, and stick to the cranes and the cargo, the brothel and the workers' meeting-place. These would provide colour for a novel in the mode of today. 'O Proletaria! stern and wild, Meet nurse for a poetic child!' Like—I thought, examining my pile of unread Penguins—like John Braine whose portrait was reproduced on the back of his *Room at the Top*, looking very much a 'poetic child'.

But this book was a surprise, one of the most startling during all this chance-led reading, and I resolved never again to form a preconception from reviews and hearsay.

I expected it to be that forbidding thing, a consciously experimental novel. Perhaps a turgid stream of consciousness would flow among the dark satanic mills. It would be bitterly satirical, I was sure, the strident voice of an angry young man speaking a crude jeremiad. Or it might be one of those shabby and obscure bits of writing that come, usually, from Australia. I had lived and read my way through back-to-the-mill periods in fiction; I remembered Gilbert Cannan, Arnold Bennett, and Wells, or later Rhys Davies, H. E. Bates and love on the dole in the 'thirties. I could not take more anguished miners and bench-hands.

I found, at first with relief, then, as I read, with delight, a fine novel in the very main highway of English fiction. Here is a writer as modern as atomic energy and all that, as adventurous as a space-traveller, a writer who has left behind his contemporaries yet who has known how to use what has gone before him, who does not suppose that good writing comes from the illiterate air, who is, in fact, that old-fashioned thing, a stylist.

Why was I not prepared for this? I had heard, heaven knows, enough about this novel and its importance as a landmark, its impatience with the world of today, its significance as an indictment of a social system in the form of a tender and moving story. Did no one notice its prose? Or is the very word outmoded? I know and respect the old critic's saw that theme and expression are indivisible, so one no more notices the quality of the writing than the colour of the binding. But a dog's coat is indivisible from the living dog yet can be considered as a coat, and sometimes a writer's prose is so unflaggingly right, so adequate to every phase of his theme, so spare and taut, so perfectly muscled that it compels admiration for itself alone. Braine's idiom is modern but his gift for effect with economy, for the nail hit clean on the head, comes straight from Defoe. It leaves a litter of Victoriana and twentieth-century experiment unnoticed.

It is not, I think, strange to find this in a first novel for if it is not in the first, to some extent, at least, it will be in no other.

[69]

It is a native woodnote, or whatever Milton said. Braine may never have read Defoe, for all I know, though I feel pretty sure his reading has been wide and included Fielding. His style is his own, tempered in his own forge by a man who consciously or not had the whole past behind him, and tempered for a specific purpose—the writing of a cruel, ironic, beautiful novel.

He had a theme and within the theme a story. Literary luck might have given him one or the other but the combination is of genius. Neither in itself is new; but what is? The theme is the stinking old world and its corruption, not (unless I overrate the author) a particular system, still less a particular national system. I say this because with only minor changes the book could have been set in Russia or America and have lost nothing by it. It could have been set in the past and—ironically enough —in the future. The theme is eternal and universal, only the story is contemporary and English. Both are developed to the full, to the very last breath. Nothing is missed, nothing is spared, and there is nothing more to be said. For once here is a novel which exhausts its subject instead of the reader.

But there is more to it than that. There is something of a miracle as well as a feat. From beginning to end of this long novel there is not a sentence, not a word, not a small incident, not one of those tempting asides that all writers know, nothing at all which is not directly relevant, which does not develop the theme or advance the story. This, in a first novel, *is* miraculous. Admittedly, the author gave himself wide terms of reference, but wide as they were they were wholly within his powers. Indeed they fitted his powers, I think, perhaps inflated them a little, but never escaped from them. How his fellow-novelists must have envied him that, when they first read this book, and how I envy him now. To achieve such complete fulfil-ment, to be able to use everything, every talent, memory, flick of imagination, every gift, vice, experience in him and to

[70]

know that he had done it—for forty years who, on this side of the Atlantic at least, has achieved that?

Of the minor skills it is not necessary to speak. Of the climax which escapes contrivance by a hair's breadth but none the less escapes it, of the compassion which is kept to a telling undertone, of the cruelty which stings but does not offend, of the stark reality of the whole thing which never allows the reader a moment's smugness but never descends to either propaganda or pornography, surely enough must have been said.

The book left me with a feeling of exaltation. There's life yet in that old performing dog the English novel, I thought as I finished it. There's even spirit, and new spirit at that. From the cold Ligurian Sea, from the frozen Gulf of Genoa, I raised an isolated *Salute* as I laid the book down.

3

Genoa under its hills, seen through the port-hole of the steam-heated saloon in which I had been reading, had meanwhile become more urgently inviting and when at last we tied up, again not alongside but stern to, I hailed a rowing-boat to take me ashore. I had a long walk through dockland before I found a taxi driven by a middle-aged man of seafaring type. Almost immediately he began to ask questions of the kind which enables the garrulous to mount their own hobbyhorses.

Had I come from the Yugoslav ship? Yes. Which way had I taken? Which way? Yes, through the docks? I did not know. Had I noticed the docks? Yes, they seemed very large. This brought a smile thrown back to me over the shoulder.

After a pause my defences were probed from another angle.

Did I know Marseilles? Yes, fairly well. The docks? Yes. Did I think they were large? Very.

The taxi was pulled into the side of the road and stopped to give the driver full scope to make his point.

'They are not as large as Genoa's,' he said triumphantly. 'Genoa has the largest docks in the Mediterranean. There are people. . .' a gesture dismissed them as credulous fools. 'There are people who think the Marseilles docks are larger. They are not. I know. *I have been there!*'

I had asked him to go to the Piazza Verdi which seemed to be central, but I began to wonder when we should reach it. Some comment was expected from me before our journey could be resumed.

'*Molto interresante,*' I tried.

'You don't believe me?' he asked hopefully.

'Yes. Yes. I believe you.'

'It's true! Genoa is larger. More important.'

'We are going to the Piazza Verdi,' I reminded him tentatively.

'Yes. I know. There are dry docks here. The shipbuilding yards of Ansaldo build cruisers. Marseilles? Nothing. Nothing.'

'The Piazza Verdi,' I said more firmly.

'Are you in a hurry?' he asked with sudden concern.

'Well. . .'

'*Andiamo!*'

We went.

4

The Piazza Verdi is a wide open space among new buildings but from it one has an uninterrupted view of the Ligurian Alps standing above Genoa. This was dramatic in the pale sunlight of that afternoon for the bright outline of the hills against a woolly white sky made them seem close to the city, fatherly white-bearded gods smiling on the buildings at their feet.

I began walking up the Via Vente Settembre and thought it one of the finest streets of its kind in Europe. This may well show a bourgeois and conventional taste in town architecture for I have loved some rather odd streets including Bombay's Marine Drive, the Calle Florida in Beunos Aires and the Promenade in Cheltenham. This one seemed to be contemporary with the Champs-Elysées—indeed there was a triumphal arch at one end of it—and built in the same florid and spacious style, but it had the wide arcades which so many Italian cities have kept or copied from earlier periods. (Our own, most lovely of all, John Nash's graceful arcade in Regent Street was destroyed by vandals in the 1920s.) Thus with wide pavements arcaded twenty feet or more high, the Via Vente Settembre sweeps from one open piazza to another, from the Arch of Victory and the Ponte Pila to the Piazza Deferrari, the true centre of the city. Its arcades are lined with shop windows rather lavishly and extravagantly filled and it has an air of prosperity.

Between it and the Via Dante I found a magnificent bookshop. London may have a few to compare with it, and perhaps Oxford or Edinburgh, but the condition of publishing and bookselling in England, brought to ruin by the Free Library, cannot allow this sort of luxurious display. Entering by a wide passage which curved for eight or ten yards between the shop's own plate-glass windows, in which books were shown abundantly but cunningly to tempt the passers-by, I came into a large hall, brilliantly lit, well but not overheated and filled with books in orderly rows. There was no crowding between shelves, no precarious ladder-climbing, no stooping to floor level.

[73]

There were plenty of assistants who knew their business and spoke, I gathered, several languages, but did not intrude on a customer who wanted to search and browse for himself.

This was a shop for new books only and the English section had a display of recently published books which could match many in Great Britain. I had no difficulty in finding half a dozen new Penguins and only the need to keep my baggage down prevented me from buying other books. When I thought of Italian bookshops before the war, or for that matter book-shops in provincial France and Germany, I understood why British authors must now look on their translation rights as a means of subsistence. Whereas before 1939 these produced a welcome but inconsiderable extra, often no more than twenty or thirty pounds for a book in another language, they now mean a substantial part of a writer's income and one at least of my books has earned me more in translations than in English.

5

I came to the city each day while we were in dock, did a little sight-seeing of a casual kind, had some good food and found my way about even in the alleys and stairways of Genova Vecchia where many streets are barred to traffic. Neither the cold, which remained pitiless, nor my solitude depressed me.

Perhaps because I had not long finished my biography of Lord Alfred Douglas I remembered Wilde's associations with Genoa. He loved it and at one time, after his imprisonment, planned to live there. He visited it first as an undergraduate and described it as 'a beautiful city of marble palaces over the sea'. His wife died in Genoa a year after his release from prison, having forbidden him to visit her there, and three years later

Wilde visited her grave in the Protestant cemetery, 'a garden at the foot of the lovely hills which girdle Genoa'. Wilde was deeply moved, though his name was not mentioned on the tombstone, and it brought from him one of those sudden out-bursts of sincerity which break tragically through his ornate prose. 'I was deeply affected—with a sense, also, of the useless-ness of all regrets. Nothing could have been otherwise, and Life is a very terrible thing.'

But the city had happier memories for him. When he and Bosie were making their escape to Naples they spent a day in Genoa, and twenty months before his death Wilde stopped there on his way to Switzerland and 'met a beautiful young actor, a Florentine, whom I wildly loved'. He had 'the strange name of Didaco' and 'a face chiselled for high romance'. Ross stayed with him in Genoa and persuaded him to drink less, afterwards paying his hotel bill.

I was not, however, looking for literary associations or I might have tried to find the Casa Saluzzo in which Byron spent his last year in Italy with Teresa Guiccioli and wrote most of *Don Juan*, or the Casa Negroto where he settled the Leigh Hunts with their seven children.

I was not, in fact, looking for anything in particular, and when I came on the cathedral it gave me a heart-leap. That astonishing façade of black and white marble in horizontal stripes over three magnificent arched doorways, that towering campanile with its modest brother—it was a grand and dramatic exterior which kept me staring like a gaby from across the way. Other churches in Genoa were older, one other at least, S. Matteo, the church of the Doria family, was more often recommended to sightseers, but this had all one could ask of a church seen from outside. It was being built while the Normans were invading England and was consecrated in 1118, yet there is something almost sophisticated in its black and white Pisan

F

style, in the elaborately carved arches of the doors and in that high campanile with its stunted fellow.

When I entered there was no disappointment—a great bare colourless nave, with a chancel like a casket of jewels. The church was not cold and it was as though that blaze of gold and colour in the east warmed its long aisles. The chancel roof was a fresco and behind the bronze altar was a gilt reredos, this concentration of colour and light was brilliant seen from the west end, a true holy of holies beyond the stern cold nave. I sat watching this as though it were the stage of a vast mediaeval theatre, and I daresay there are those who would find it more theatrical than beautiful. Afterwards I would not go to the cathedral treasury where an old glass octagonal bowl, the Sacro Catino, is kept though it is no longer claimed to be either an emerald or the Holy Grail as once it was. Instead I put a coin in an ingenious form of pick-up with earphones which played a record describing the cathedral in the language of your choice. How much better than the ignorant and expensive guides who lie in wait in English cathedrals.

That visit to the cathedral of S. Lorenzo was enough of sight-seeing, though the 'Venus and Mars' of Rubens, with that beautiful blowsy woman whose breast is pinched by a splendid absent-minded cavalier, was in one gallery and one of Van Cleve's loveliest Madonnas in another.

I used to lunch each day in a restaurant just off the Vente Settembre which had been recommended to me by a book-seller as one of the best in the town. I daresay it was, and though I might have found better food or more elegant surroundings, I remained faithful to it throughout our stay in port. It was called the Bolognese like so many good restaurants up and down Italy, for it seems that Bologna was a gastronomical centre almost before it became a university town in the eleventh century. It manufactures sausage—*mortadella Bolognese* is famous—and *tortellini* and a number of excellent liqueurs. Fielding speaks of Bologna sausage in *Tom Jones*. But it is perhaps claiming too much for it that it produces a type or a school of cooking.

The Italians like to remember the supposed regional origins of their dishes and *alla Romana, alla Milanese, alla Fiorentina, alla Veneziana, alla Napoletana* and so on occur in nearly all their menus. Bologna is not forgotten and often when sausages are used in the preparation of a dish we find *alla Bolognese*, which is also used for a simple but succulent preparation of tunny fish. The only use I knew for the name of the town I was in was *salsa Genovese* for an excellent sharp sauce for boiled fish.

To the Italians we owe a great debt in the matter of cooking for it was they who kept the art alive through the Dark Ages and there are dishes in Italy which go straight back to Rome. In the great days of the Renaissance gastronomy as an art and a science reached a level seldom seen and accounts of banquets in Venice in the sixteenth century show something more than the absurd profusion of historical banquets elsewhere, show understanding and taste and discrimination. Not till 1553 when Catherine de Medici took her cooks to France and set a new fashion at the royal court, did the French awaken to this. It is to me a pleasant experience to eat something which may have been cooked in this way in certain regions for five hundred or even perhaps two thousand years. The history of cooking has yet to be written and until someone is prepared to devote his lifetime to research we cannot know whether the cooks of the Roman legions made *minestra* or *polenta* or what Trimulcio ate when he was not feasting.

Meanwhile I ate well at the Bolognese and regretted its direct, unelaborate, perfectly timed cooking when at last we sailed for Naples.

6

NAPLES

We were at sea for a day and a night between Genoa and Naples but with time spent on board waiting to sail, and time before I could go ashore, I had the best part of three days in which to read, and a stack of bright new Penguins to choose from. First I decided on *Homecomings* by C. P. Snow which I read conscientiously and attentively.

It puzzled me a great deal until I decided that the fault, the blindness, the obtuseness were mine. I must have missed some quality which had given this, and the other novels in Snow's sequence, its prestige and acclaim. It could not possibly be the commonplace thing it seemed to me.

Or was I prejudiced? An uncomfortable thought. I had once been acquainted with Snow before his knighthood and marriage, and before his premature candidateship for literary Grand Old Manhood. Even then he was Old Snow to me and others who knew him, wise Old Snow, knowledgeable Old Snow, rather talkative Old Snow, who watched his press-cuttings, made his contracts, had his elations and reverses like

[78]

the rest of us. His appearance was a mite ecclesiastical, his conversation generalized and rather pointedly above gossip, but he had a friendly laugh and not more pomposity than any other senior civil servant. True, there was not much indication of the Important Figure to come but writers no longer show, if they ever did, the accoutrements of genius on their persons. The man I knew was as likely as anyone else to write a good book and from estimates of him in the weeklies and intellectual Sunday newspapers I assumed later that he had done so. I remembered a hot June night during a week-end in Suffolk when a number of us lay on freshly cut hay and listened to Snow discoursing rather imaginatively on the stars above us. Something of the quality of his talk that night must be in his books, I supposed, when I read that *The Times* thought him 'the exponent of a new literary movement'. Nor had I anything but admiration for his aplomb and circumspection in dropping what acquaintance he had with me at the time and in the manner which best suited him, a step which afterwards showed his foresight. I thought him, in fact, shrewd and rather formidable. No, it was not prejudice but my own dull inability to respond or appreciate which caused me to look back helplessly over *Homecomings* when I had finished it that night outside Genoa.

I had been prepared to dislike it, of course, but that was another matter. I did not dislike the book but failed to find anything in it to dislike or greatly admire. I knew that as a writer Snow cuts critical opinion sharply in two. He has his adherents who are impressed by the cycle of long books he devotes to the sex-and-soul life (as with his liking for such hyphenated combinations he might well have called it) of a single character. He also has his vocal denigrators who find Lewis Eliot frankly tiresome. Whether or not he has that casual healthy following of interested but not adulatory readers who say of a writer

'Well, I quite like *some* things he has written', I do not know. It would seem that in most public critical opinion he is either a genius or a bore and I had read *Homecomings* to find out which I thought him. My bewilderment, my disappointment was caused because he seemed to me neither, and I could *not* see what all the fuss has been about.

For however many novels like this there may be in the series that Snow has planned and partly executed, how can it have been solemnly wagged over as a literary event? It is intelligent, of course, the prose is careful and one is never allowed quite to lose interest in the chattering characters moving about between their London offices, pubs, lodgings, bedrooms, flats and parties, but what on earth is there to justify either the fanfares of newspaper critics or the high-toned disapproval of F. R. Leavis?

The novel records the life of a senior civil servant in wartime told chiefly in a series of humdrum dialogues between the man and his associates male and female, with interpolations to explain motives or call attention to facial expressions or vocal undertones. Instead of imaginative interpretation there is rather morbid introspection, instead of incident there are fussy movements and over-observed contacts, instead of realism there is verisimilitude. It was clearly the author's purpose to ignore the war and this might have been bold and effective but becomes almost silly when in one of the few oblique references to life in London during the blitz we learn that Lewis Eliot's breakfast had 'reached the irreducible minimum, a small pot of tea and a biscuit'. Instead of comedy, *any* comedy, there is a landlady with a trick of speech as remorselessly repetitive as Mr Micawber's, while instead of tragedy there is the insignificant suicide of a psychopathic wife and, as a grand climax, the dangerous illness of a small child.

The record is of adulteries and divorces, minutes and debates at the Ministry, appointments in cafés, clubs and pubs, tickling pieces of relationship between minor characters, small disappointments and endless psychological tittle-tattle. When the author in his didactic prose comes to give, with a defiant air of I-can-do-this-too, details of sexual contacts between his characters it is nothing short of embarrassing. When he pops in bits of chatter between his Chelsea-ites or government officials, when he pairs off his characters or reports their infidelities, when he devotes his short chapters, each scrupulously titled, to some by-play among in-laws or secretaries, all seen with meticulous fidelity to details of behaviour but never in depth, I find it hard to plod on.

So with no attempt at sarcasm but in all sincerity I say that I must be missing something, must be blind or tone-deaf. Criticism, favourable or unfavourable to Snow's novels, has for years started with the certainty that they are more than the lucubrations of a highly intelligent man over a number of cleverly conceived everyday characters, a report of human dramatics rather than drama, and this is all that one of them, *Homecomings*, seems to me. I can appreciate its well-informed precision, I can admire its avoidance of the outsize, but I cannot for the life of me see more.

2

I went straight from one booming reputation to another and read *The End of the Affair* by Graham Greene.

This must be one of the few living novelists who can reread his early books without suffocating embarrassment. His first, *The Man Within*, was astonishingly deft and mature and made him a seriously considered writer at once, and he never, as they

[*81*]

say, looked back in public estimation. Moreover, his books soon attracted film producers, a more rewarding kind of popularity. He has had what is called a brilliant career which is all the more laudable for being an exclusively literary one.

That, to me, is the thing. I have a respect not only for the art but for the profession of writing. I have no respect at all for the amateur, unless he is impatiently on his way to professionalism. Or for people who 'do a little writing in their spare time', television entertainers, radio performers, company directors, dons and schoolmasters who 'would like to write more but can't afford to devote themselves to it'. I firmly believe that the dry-rot in modern letters began to spread when men and women were no longer satisfied to write for a living. (That Kenneth Grahame may be quoted as the prime exception means nothing. He was an exception to most rules.)

Forty years ago, when far less books were published, the number of professional novelists in Great Britain must have run into four figures, now it would be hard to name a hundred who are, in a significant catch-term, whole-time writers. Yet the writing profession was no less precarious then and it was probably harder to get a first novel published. A few truly professional writers survive from that time, and a few who started then and have never been diverted. But those who came afterwards grow less and in the generation of Evelyn Waugh, Graham Greene, and H. E. Bates only a few successful ones survive as writers—the rest have gone whoring with their own inventions, while in the post-war generation there is not much sign of constancy to letters. It has doubtless an economic cause for it becomes more and more difficult for anyone to live by writing books unless he is prepared to show himself in the side-shows of the profession. A dismal prospect.

Graham Greene started in the classic way by publishing a book of verse while still an undergraduate, then getting a job on a newspaper before his first novel came out in his twenty-fifth year. He made some experiments in his early books, he travelled widely, he has an interest in publishing, but letters have been his life. From such a man it can be expected that his best will be his best, and he has a wry way of categorizing some of his books as 'entertainments', as if to warn his reader that with such an output—he has published more than thirty novels—he must at times relax.

The End of the Affair is not listed as an entertainment and so must be considered as entertainment plus. It is a curious book and not altogether a satisfying one.

If a huge literary award were offered for the best rendering of Francis Thompson's *The Hound of Heaven* as fiction, the resulting novels are all too foreseeable. They would read like those cosy stories of conversion, or repentance, or a rectified lapse, or an avoided mixed marriage, which used to appear—and may still for all I know—in periodicals like *The Catholic Fireside* or *The Irish Rosary*. They would be chatty and comforting and help not very intelligent people to bear affliction. But if an accomplished novelist, who had written powerful stories on very different themes, were to enter the competition the result might be this book.

It is a story of conversion, and as such it fails as literature though it succeeds as—there is no other word—propaganda. It has this in common with all stories of conversion from St Paul's onward. Inexplicable, that. Conversion should be a splendid theme for the novelist or historian but they both fall down on it. The calling of the disciples, a superb piece of economic narrative, is not a story of conversion but of a personal summons obeyed. It has no suggestion of an immediate change of creed or sudden new understanding by the young peasants addressed and if it had these the tale would be ruined. They were called, they followed, accepting leadership, feeling

[83]

love and bewildered faith, but they were not converted when they left their lives and possessions and became, as they thought, the bodyguard of a dangerous idealist. Conversion and understanding came afterwards and is assumed, not described in the gospels.

What could be more tempting than conversion as a theme? To a certain kind of novelist, concerned with thought and emotion, the development of character, conflict of mind, the grindstone of the will, it offers everything. It is potentially full of battle and crisis, of thrilling suspense, of victory or failure. Yet no one, not even the hagiologists, not even St Augustine, not even Newman, has made it a literary success.

Graham Greene's was a brave try. His book is written with consummate skill, with a sincerity which is never mawkish or sentimental and as a love-story it is cruelly convincing. The author is persuasive, yet keeps his own balance. It is not that we do not believe him—there is not a lie in the book. But there was a foretaste of failure in it, and all his arts cannot expel it.

Obviously propaganda can be literature, but can it be good fiction? We buy and read this, after all, as a novel by a man who is a master of the craft, and as a novel it is a bit of a sell. It did not take the whole author to write it. It took the skilled technician, the practised writer with shrewd insight and keen imagination who knew just where he was going and what he could do, who could touch with significant sorcery the smallest detail and incident and who, above all, could make us feel with his characters. But it leaves us wanting more.

Perhaps that is Graham Greene's secret. Perhaps it is his weakness, too. He always leaves us wanting more and believing that he can and will give it in his next book. Perhaps that is why he has been, and still is, one of the best hopes of the present barren age. He seems always on the verge of great achievement and no one who reads his novels doubts that he is capable of it.

It has been so from his first book. Then what, I ask myself miserably as I finish *The End of the Affair*, what if after all he has no more to give? What if I was wrong in suggesting that it did not take the whole writer to create this? What if the supreme achievement is never to come? What if he is the one-book author who fails to produce the one book?

Nonsense. It will come. Let's wait for the next.

3

The run from Genoa to Naples brought us unmistakably to the south. It has been said that the southern parts of all countries in the northern hemisphere have much in common, in terrain and humanity, and this has been accounted for by their greater proximity to the Equator. The Spaniard of Andalucia, the Frenchman of the Midi, the Italian of Campania and Calabria, the Greek of Peloponnesos, the Indian of Madras, are supposed to share a greater agility of mind, more sexual abandon, less substance and worth than their northern neighbours, besides being darker and more vivid in physical type. It has even been suggested that these qualities correspond, in a suitably modified way, in England where the solid men of Yorkshire and the north consider the southerner from round London a wily and meretricious creature.

It is an attractive theory, particularly as it goes into the reverse in the southern hemisphere with the dark and wily ones nearer the Equator in the north, and the bluff business types, the Argentines as compared with the Venezuelans, in the south.

It is hard to see how thirty-six hours' steaming in the Mediterranean can make all that difference, however; all the difference, I mean, which was at once perceptible when we

[85]

reached Naples. The landscape we watched while approaching, the city seen from the decks, the people who crowded on board, were all 'southern' in aspect and the air seemed less frozen.

Coming into a long-awaited port has always been for me a dramatic thing and I could remember a score of occasions; the approach to Boulogne on my first crossing the Channel, to Coruña, Lisbon, Rio de Janeiro, Hamburg, Cadiz, Durban. But most vivid of all was the approach to Bombay, for then I was coming to the East. In all Conrad there is nothing that speaks so directly to me as that passage in *Youth* when Marlow, after a marine Pilgrim's Progress, first saw the East, and when I came to it on a lousy troopship in 1943 I would let nothing spoil my enjoyment of it.

It was, I remembered on that Neapolitan morning, twenty years earlier, certainly to the month, perhaps to the day. We were confined to a troopdeck from which it was impossible to see even the Gateway of India and to pass the time and to amuse my friend Little Arthur (who was six foot three and a cockney unaccountably serving with the Royal Scots Fusiliers) I conducted a small Gallup Poll of my own among the men waiting among the cockroaches. 'What,' I asked each, 'is your idea of heaven?'

Apart from one notion which with variations occurred in almost half the answers, the pictures given were homely and revealing. They included the ownership of a pub that never opened and a number of rude formulae connected with the wife. There were whimsical answers involving the production of photographs from wallets, and poetic ones like lying by a running stream with a gallon of old ale. There were curt nostalgic ones like being back in Glasgow, rambling ones about excursions to Blackpool and exasperated ones like being off this bloody ship.

But it was Little Arthur who gave the most popular answer,

the one which had already emerged incoherently in wistful tones from a dozen others. It was Little Arthur who summed it up.

'Lying in bed on Sunday morning with a cup of tea and the *News of the World.*'

After that nobody made any new suggestions but said— 'That's about it, I reckon.' 'That would do for me.' Or, 'What Little Arthur said.' So my poll was a success.

But when I went to see Little Arthur twelve years later I did not remind him of it and I soon found, with no surprise at all, that he had forgotten that conversation on board. He came to the door of his neat little house and without asking me in said 'Half a minute. I'll get my cap.'

I caught a glimpse of a trim interior and a tidy little woman with tight lips, also a number of leggy schoolgirls but Little Arthur seemed in a hurry. When we had sunk our first pints he looked reflective and said, 'Well, I dunno.'

I knew this statement to be introductory like 'Once upon a time. . .' or 'Have you heard the one about. . .' So I waited.

'Three daughters,' grumbled Little Arthur. 'Always wanting something.'

I looked sympathetic.

'Then there's the wife,' said Little Arthur, and stopped again. He had aged somewhat but seemed if anything taller and heavier.

'It's a bastard, isn't it?' he finished.

'What about Sunday mornings?' I asked. 'Manage to stay in bed?'

'What do *you* think?' asked Little Arthur.

'Get your cup of tea?'

'There'd be trouble if I didn't.'

'*News of the World* delivered all right?'

'Oh yes,' said Little Arthur without enthusiasm or any idea where I was leading him.

'Three girls,' he repeated sourly. 'And the wife.'

'Tell me, Little Arthur,' I said. 'What's your idea of heaven?'

'Mine? I'll tell you. Being on a flaming troopship nearing Bombay. That's my idea, if you want to know.'

It was neat and ironic and Little Arthur added gravely, 'Makes you think, doesn't it?'

It did. And because Little Arthur and his friends had more natural wisdom than I had, I examined his answers, and all the other answers I had collected, to see what they had in common. It was obvious enough. They all wanted something they had once had and lost. They did not look forward to heaven, for attempts to imagine a heaven to look forward to have been notable failures, except perhaps for wholesale jewellers. They looked back on it. To Eden, in fact, where they were all at home.

4

But this was Naples I was approaching, not Bombay, Naples which, say the guidebooks, disputes only with Istanbul the claim to occupying the most beautiful site in Europe. I do not know why I thought of Bombay which has little to show those coming from the sea either of architecture or of natural beauty. Perhaps because Bombay is the gateway of the Orient and Naples that of another region no less full of legend, no less part of our child's world of imagination. *Campania Felix*, Vesuvius, Herculaneum, Pompeii, Naples itself, a rich and bloody pageant of history stretching back to the first Greek settlement at Ischia.

We had entered the bay before daylight but in the bright early morning I saw the city rising like an amphitheatre from the sea, as millions of sightseers had before me, but as I myself had done once only, then at dusk. From St Elmo down to the promontory it seemed an ancient city on which modern buildings intruded, rather than a new city treasuring a few antiquities.

The ship grew crowded with that congregation of officials and hangers-on which invade ships everywhere but nowhere more than in southern Italy. There were at least thirty of them, customs officers, police, laundrymen, barbers, watchmen, guides, all asking the Chief Steward for free cigarettes, all good-tempered and noisy. I was impatient to go ashore, already responsive to the atmosphere.

But there was a disappointment. The *Trepča* would be only a few hours in port, so the Chief Steward told me of mysterious instructions from the bridge. I must be on board by three o'clock that afternoon.

This meant that with time to see so little I should see nothing at all of one of the world's greatest treasure-houses. Pompeii I knew, at least with a leisurely tourist's knowledge, from thirty years earlier and it was almost as vividly in my mind as then. I had once made my pilgrimage to Vergil's tomb, and to that of S. Gennaro in the modern-faced cathedral. But today I had intended to go to the National Museum which houses the greatest archaeological collection in Europe, from Italo-Greek to the eighteenth century. I consoled myself with the reflection that it would take weeks to know anything of this alone, and it was one of a score of museums and galleries, while there are 237 churches in the city and 57 chapels, most of which have the rich internal decoration I unashamedly love.

No, all or nothing. I would take a walk, chancing my way through the smaller streets, having a drink in the Galeria which had for me the warmest memories, lunching somewhere near by and returning by the Via Roma which, I remembered, is always called Toledo. In England we use our nicknames for streets officially, like Piccadilly and Pall Mall, but in Naples and Madrid, and perhaps in other Italian and Spanish cities, the more ostentatious names have a familiar and unchanging version. Thus no one in Madrid asks for the Avenida José Antonio Primo de Rivero but simply for the Gran Via, while in Naples the Via Roma is Toledo.

I would, in fact, feel myself back in Naples, sniff it and watch the street-scene and be satisfied with that. I am no antiquarian, anyway, and though I like to see history in things, I would rather get a sense of the place and its people and see how closely it resembled the city I remembered.

As soon as I entered the narrower streets of tall houses I was at home. This was the Naples I knew—washing hanging from the balconies to catch a sidelong streak of winter sunlight, booths in the street, crowds chattering at the tops of their voices, laughing, cadging, bargaining, begging, but begging without earnestness or determination as though to seize a passing chance. A woman sang from a balcony absent-mindedly yet powerfully, like a prima donna in a highly produced film. A quarrel broke out vehemently in a group round a doorway —or was it only an argument? There was less poverty visible than of old, but more than in the north.

It was cold, though. From our own literature of Italy one would suppose that the country never knew a frosty day or even a rainy one. That torrent of sunshine which pours on the pages of every novel and blisters every guidebook is as much a part of Italy as her churches and cypresses, her olives and vines. But hell, it can freeze up all the *dolce far niente*, it can make the carefree peasantry purposeful blue-nosed people hurrying about their business. There was sunlight this morning which brought a light gleam of gaiety into the air, but these cavernous streets could be dreary in a long-enduring rainstorm or in an early dusk.

I found the Galeria as gilt and absurd, as like a misplaced Crystal Palace, as I remembered it, but there was no lounging promenade of pomaded young men on this busy morning, only a few quick coffee-drinkers or readers of newspapers. It was out of the wind, though, and I had known it in belated adolescence and came to sit in it like a faithful churchgoer. There had been a novel about it since those days—or was Moravia writing of another gallery? There had also been a war and an invasion and this was no summer evening which stretched invitingly ahead.

I lunched on *zuppa di pesce* and thought it no better than some of the fish soups of Spain but preferable to the restaurant versions of *bouillabaisse* one is given in Marseilles. Then *vermicelli alle congole* with cockles in tomato sauce which the waiter assured me was a famous Neapolitan dish. A veal cutlet, deliciously tender, and a cream cheese called Mascherone which I did not know previously but found soft and delicate, finished my only Neapolitan meal.

5

My last impression of Naples, formed as I was driven back to the ship, was of an eighteenth-century city of elegance and grandeur, of great palaces with interminable regular façades like a plastered Versailles. What a city it must have been as the capital of the Two Sicilies when the gardens of the Villa Nazionale were first laid out in 1780, when the Palazzo Reale was indeed a Royal Palace, a city of carriages and finery and grinning poverty where love could be bought for a copper coin and intrigue ran down from the court to the gutters. It is still remotely, by suggestion, that kind of place—at least the last glories of a gorgeous

G

epoch remain in its buildings. Poverty? Slavery? What beauty has man ever created without them?

We sailed at five o'clock and it was good to find the evening longer here so that I could see the bay as we left it. Vesuvius had nothing on the sun for sheer theatrical effect, for the sun was a dull flame-coloured ball in a dim pearly sky which made the landscape tremble. We came to Capri, passing through the narrow strait between it and Punta della Campanella.

I find among some papers a short and enigmatic note on this which suggests that I was a trifle light-headed when I wrote it, either from the beauty of the scene or Scotch whisky. 'Capri from here long low with four humps. Street-lights visible high up in the centre. Probably Blackpool ashore but from here soft slate-grey and romantic. Its history credible in this light— Tiberius to Fersen. Shall never visit it. That's enough.'

The meaning of the last two sentences I cannot even guess. So far from being determined not to visit Capri I have always had an idea that it is less overrun, vulgarized and beastly than report has increasingly made it out in the last forty years. Though the sirens and the Roman ghosts have gone and San Michele is an empty memorial to the garrulous old gentlemen who owned it, there must still be traces of that lost world described by Norman Douglas and Roger Peyrefitte, the little world of Count d'Adelsward Fersen and Nino Cesarini, of the Café Morgano and the Hotel Quisisana, of Ephy Lovatelli and the Misses Wolcott-Perry, and the rest of that exotic company whose adventures, under the names chosen for them by several novelists, I had followed, but nowhere more hilariously or affectionately than in Mackenzie's nostalgic masterpiece *Vestal Fire*.

However, 'that's enough' I had written of Capri and perhaps in the circumstances and for the present I was right.

7

CATANIA

From Italy to Sicily, from Naples to Catania, from Vesuvius to Etna, one great volcano to another—for this journey I wanted something large and powerful to read and I found it in *For Whom the Bell Tolls*.

I knew Hemingway only slightly as man and writer and disliked him as both. As a man he seemed anxious to stress an excessive virility, to shoulder aside less pugnacious spirits and to proclaim himself lover, pioneer, hunter, deep-sea fisherman, bull-fighter, traveller, all hardy and masculine things, rather than a mere hard-working novelist. He reminded me of George Borrow, who had the same obsession, until I was forced to wonder whether it was from the same cause—for Borrow was sexually impotent. Hemingway's frequent expressed detestation of homosexuals might well be, I thought, a kind of envy for their vigorous promiscuity.

This was also perceptible in such of his work as I had read. All his geese were swans and each of his women was Leda. His males did not behave with the priapic and wordy abandon of

[93]

the men in D. H. Lawrence's novels but with a tacit lustfulness which was Hemingway's own. They had to fight in a war or climb a mountain or undergo fierce privations manfully before they were rewarded with the willing bodies of women. It was an artificial business and I found it tiresome and arty, which was exactly what it was meant not to be.

But then I had not read the Spanish novels—*Death in the Afternoon* or *For Whom the Bell Tolls*.

Why hadn't I? There had been opportunities enough. In various places and at various times I had picked up one or the other and after reading a little put it down, impatient, even irritated. I did not admit not having read them and if asked—and who has not been asked in these past twenty years?—'what I thought of' Hemingway, I would say he was overrated, which was true enough at the beginning of his career when *Farewell to Arms* received an acclaim it never deserved.

I suppose I was jealous. Not, I must say at once, of his success or his sales. I have envied no writer these, for it has always seemed to me such a happy miracle that I should be able to live by writing at all that I have never felt jealousy of those who not only earn a living but become rich through the practice of this profession. It was another kind of envy and connected with Spain.

For I too loved Spain and when I was young wanted to write about it. I too knew bull-fighters and the Spanish landscape, and the people under succeeding regimes—a monarchy, a republic, an anarchy, and the regime of today. I had that peculiar vanity which is a vice with so many English hispanophils, that my Spain was the real one, that I understood the Spaniard and what not. I wrote a novel called *Picaro* which was set half in Spain, half in Argentina, a book which I then fancied mightily and which even today seems the least shoddy and over-written of my early books. But I knew it was not half the book I could, and one day should, write about Spain. Then before I could compass that, here was Hemingway who had, I was given to understand on all sides, gloriously got away with it, made something like a corner in Spain and the Spanish. No doubt it was petty and mean-spirited to feel like that but I did so for several years, creating an anti-Hemingway crust which became a habit until it was forgotten in the war and events since then.

So when I found *For Whom the Bell Tolls* in Naples I bought it with what are called mixed feelings. But when I had finished it I realized the till-now-incredible truth, that this was one of the great novels of all time. I realized, too, that I was a bit late in making the discovery, that my news was stale and my wonderment outdated. For all I know reaction has already set in and Hemingway may be considered *passé*. What does it matter? His reputation lasted his life, and time and tide wait for every man, sweeping back and forth interminably. If he is 'out' now he'll be 'in' again in fifty or five hundred years, if literature survives.

Why, I ask myself, on the strength of a single book—for that's what it comes to—can I be sure of this. Most qualities in *For Whom the Bell Tolls* have been surpassed by other modern books. In one, admittedly a narrow, sense it is not particularly 'well written'. There is some hideous syntax in it and one is frequently offended by phrases like 'in the house outside of the Escorial' and 'Robert Jordan's luck held very good'—not in the dialogue but in the author's own narrative. The book is informed by a gross and not always intelligent fatalism. The central character exists only as a central character, never in his own right or as a recognizable or even imaginable human being. Some of the love scenes are protracted into absurdity.

But there it is, with *The Brothers Karamazov* and *Lord Jim*, *Henry Esmond*, *Don Quixote*, *David Copperfield* and the rest

[*95*]

chosen according to your faith and reasoning, but certainly there, certainly sure of its place, high or low in the category as you please, but without a doubt a great novel.

I think it is the inevitability, the sureness and rightness, the clear and absolute necessity of every word of dialogue, every character, every minute incident, every line of description, the wholeness and economy of the book which is its strength. Nothing is superfluous to the whole, nothing could be added. It is created, not written. It is flawless in conception and its faults as a structure only emphasize that.

The action of the book falls within four days, with some perfectly assimilated flashbacks. This in itself is not remarkable, but within those days is concentrated the whole tragedy of a civil war and a nation in agony. More, too. The war and the nation are in a sense incidental, for this is Gehenna and all humanity is involved. Hemingway never stoops to symbolism, his characters are not types and the events he describes, even the most lethal of them, are almost casual in their deliberate lack of any significance except their significance in the story. The whole thing is not a microcosm, as a lesser writer might have made it. The episode which is the basis of the narrative is almost a commonplace of warfare. But it makes me remember at once that there is no symbolism in *Hamlet*, and that story too is universal, that story too in its rudiments is based on an unoriginal sequence of events.

There have been novels in plenty more artfully planned, but in them one is aware of the planning. Here there is no discernible plan at all. It is organic. It has no artificial suspense—it has actuality. It is not recounted, it happens.

It is scarcely necessary to speak of its minor excellences. The dialogue, for instance, is produced by the author thinking in Spanish as he wrote in English, producing English words with a Spanish construction. Too much of this, too literal a version of this can be disastrous. Hemingway's is natural and unstumb-lingly conveys enough idiom to reveal character, racial or individual. Again, Pilar's story of the outbreak of revolution in a village is not an anecdote within a novel but an integral part of it, actuality within actuality. Oh, and many more smaller virtues.

It reduces criticism, at least from me, almost to incoherence, to adolescent applause. I do not want to analyse greatness; in this book I recognize it, know it, feel it, am grateful for it, but cannot argue about it. And greatness is a word I like to hoard for the last Salvo.

2

This was not the way to visit Sicily for the first time. When I thought what the island had meant to civilization from the rock engravings of the Stone Age, through Greek and Roman occupation to Byzantine and later Arabian rule, its people's perpetual will to create beauty and live pleasantly undeterred by the eruptions of Etna and the murderous intrigues of the Mafia, when I remembered what it had been in literature and how many immigrant writers and artists had drawn inspiration from it, I felt it impertinent even to record a few days ashore in one of its less interesting cities.

Had I been going to Lampedusa's Palermo or to the Taor-mina of Lawrence and von Gloeden or even to Messina, I might have drawn some literary profit from the short stay, but Cat-ania is a port and the taking-off place for visits to the crater of Etna in which I had no interest, and all I could hope for was a sailor's view of Sicily, a few mental snapshots, a brief sense of being in an ancient land, perhaps, before we moved on.

Yet long before we reached its bay I was rewarded by one of the loveliest sights in the world, the Straits of Messina in the early morning with the quadruple splendour, unique in my experience, of sea, mountain, snow and sunlight. The mountains, thickly and brilliantly powdered, stood out with sharp contrasts of light and shadow behind white villages along the shore, and there was a mountain in the clouds behind these, half-revealed and mysterious in the empyreal distance. The sea was of an opaque rich blue, not a touch of green or grey near land or horizon, a uniform royal blue which made its own breakers and the white hills behind them rise luminously. As we came down the seaboard, towns sprawled along the coast and when we were alongside I looked from my porthole to see Etna framed precisely in its centre.

There was no disappointment ashore. Almost everything here was built between the time of the devastating earthquake of 1693 and the early nineteenth century, the period I most appreciate, and the modern buildings stand gauche and isolated among the grand façades.

There seemed to be no foreigners. In Italy I had heard English and seen many traces left by the northern invaders of summer, but here there was not a face, a word, a newspaper, a book, a sign *English Spoken* or a displayed souvenir that was not Sicilian. I had forgotten this when I had regretted the futility of my short visit. At least, on this last day of January, I should see Catania as itself.

And as itself it pleased me at once and continued to do so during my stay. I was given a leaflet describing in four languages the sights and wonders of the town and soon realized that the Sicilian who had turned its words into English was a wag or a poet *manqué* or simply a literalist, for some of his verbal effects were stupendous. Catania was known for 'the vastitude of the highest volcano in Europe which offers incomparable scientific and sportive charms'. The Bellini Gardens 'lofty and inspired

[98]

terraces watched over by the mass of the skyscraper, unique for its floral decorations, fortified by creepers, superb in its aspect like the swans in its fountains, but welcoming and restful in its shady walks and its tended and refined aspects'. Catania possessed 'inspired and rational modern architecture which extends, dominating the vastness of the gulf, towards the slopes of Etna with a truly impressive rhythm'. The 'majestic Bellini Theatre affirms by its perfect acoustics and resonance, with its gold and its stuccos and its frescoes that it is one of the most estimable in Italy'. The port 'receives intense sea-going traffic', the Castle of Aci,' solitary and superb, of the airy glacis, offers an almost unreal vision of the abundance of the scenery, colours and transparency which balance with perfumes, suspended in the air like constant memories of myth and legend which vibrate in every corner of the precious land which offers the most that can be desired to feed and satisfy the spirit in serene repose'.

Phew. The writer of that would be alarmed to know that one visitor at least to Catania found his interest first caught by narrow by-streets festooned with washing which he compared with those of Andalucia where the balcony is reserved for long hours of street-observation while washing dries on the roof. Homely, friendly, rich in smells, keeping some touch of summer even on this icy day, the little streets of Catania were welcoming and I did not want to hurry through them to the 'crowded and representative' Via Etnea.

This, when I found it, was remarkable for it had been built like an arrow pointing to Etna, a straight line nearly two miles long between nineteenth-century buildings with the volcano in the distance as its aim. As for Baroque—I had never seen an example so splendidly exaggerated as the collegiate church of St Nicholas of Rena, but all over the town Baroque was rampant, lavish, proliferating and beautiful. I loved it.

Sitting in a café from which I could watch the street I thought how ironic it was that I should be coming ashore here, a common sightseer, gazing at architecture and people, liking the town and its erratic tempo, enjoying myself, only twenty years after the Eighth Army had fought in these streets after the brilliant landings of Operation Husky. I could guess what the name Catania still meant in a few British and American homes, for I knew what Diego Suarez meant in even fewer. That episode will soon pass into history with Carthaginian, Roman, Arab and Norman invasions, and General Alexander's name be one with Hannibal, Sextus Pompeius, Maniaces and Roger I, a history-book name as ours becomes a history-book war. At the time it must have seemed to the people of this and other Sicilian towns that civic life itself had been destroyed and that nothing could be made of its ruins. Yet here it was unscarred and smiling with 'inspired and rational modern architecture' in a forest of Baroque.

3

I asked a taxi-driver to take me to the best restaurant and he drove me to the lofty unpromising portals of a luxury hotel. Never a lover of hotel food which has a terrible sameness in de luxe hotels all over Europe, I entered only for a drink at the bar. Here I broke the silence of days at sea (for the Chief Steward had used his little English and Boris had exhausted his life-story) in a parry-and-thrust conversation with the barman—more parry than thrust.

He was a Neapolitan, long-lashed, olive skinned, supple, yet wholly masculine, a true southerner with restless gestures, soft yet brilliant dark eyes, a quick smile and delicate strong hands. He gave me that barman's courtesy and intimacy I know so well, that act which makes each customer feel he is the one awaited with impatience and longing, that slightly whorish attentiveness turning to self-conscious independence, which I have found in the manner of many of his trade in many countries.

He was solicitous. Was I *enjoying* Catania? Only just ashore? But I must find it beautiful. Of course it wasn't like the summer, the season of *forestieri*. How was my drink? Was there anything I particularly wanted to see? To do? Would I go to Etna? A pity he had this job, he would like to accompany me. Did I like girls? Boys? They were both so abundant and so beautiful in Catania. I should see if I stayed a few days.

His melting eyes flashed. English or American? There! He had thought I was English. The English were so much better than the Americans. . . (Scarcely a waiter or a barman in Europe who hasn't learnt that nothing pleases the English, or the Americans, more than to be preferred to the other.) There were many here in the summer. Why had I not come in the summer? A better place then. The beaches! Did I like swimming? As for him, he *adored* it. He could spend his life in the water. His sweetheart grew quite angry about that. Why are you always in the water? she said. But he didn't care. He would rather swim than—almost anything. Another drink? Certainly. Delighted. Was I lunching in the hotel? No? Quite right. There were better places. He would tell me a restaurant. It was on the coast just out of the town. The Cyclops Riviera they called this coast. One moment. He must serve this customer. Only one little moment. . .

How insidious, I thought, remembering the northerners, men and women who are annually captivated by the glossy charm of such as this. Insidious because almost convincing. Only ten years ago I might have thought him pleased to see me—now I knew him pleased to see a customer.

[*101*]

His name? Gennaro. S. Gennaro was the patron saint of
Naples. This gentleman who had just come in lived near the
restaurant he was talking about. He would take me there on
his way home. No, no. He would be delighted. He was a
friend of Gennaro's. Signor Dottore, you will drop this gentleman at the Selena restaurant? It is on your way...

Gennaro beamed. Wonderful! He had arranged something.
Everyone was happy. He was happy when he had my tip, to
which I had added the taxi fare he had saved me. But he would
have been happy anyway, or at any rate smiling.

The Selena restaurant, ten miles from the town on a rocky
coast had been built with huge sheets of glass to catch the sunlight, a sort of covered terrace over the sea. It was gay and
attractive and its waiters were smiling professionals, attentive
and helpful. I ordered a *risotto* of shellfish, and rabbit in
bitter-sweet sauce because the name of the sauce tickled me,
agrodolce.

'A truly Sicilian dish,' commented the waiter and I broke my
resolve sufficiently to order a half bottle of a local wine, having
heard that the *vini dell'Etnea* were not so bad. It had a good
bouquet and gave no trouble.

4

Another day passed. I saw the Roman amphitheatre and a
great deal more Baroque architecture, avoiding interiors. I went
to another restaurant on the coast, the Nave or Ship—a huge
room laid out with what seemed acres of napery and only a
dozen customers. (*Scampi alla Americana* were a failure, the
scampi no more than fat prawns and the rice undercooked as
it often is in Spain and Italy. Europeans can't cook rice.) I

[*102*]

mooched about at night, wandering up the Via Etnea to the Café Italia which seemed the liveliest place in this off-season. I did not want to live here, I saw no reason ever to return but I was happy and at peace in Catania.

We sailed towards evening on the fourth day, passing through mist and rainstorm on our way to the Adriatic. I began to read a book which had roused my curiosity by its title, *Miss Lonelyhearts*. I remembered its first publication in England six years earlier and a great deal of talk of it at the time. I soon understood why. Here was a writer like a bull in the ring, charging madly but hopelessly at every movement of humanity in sight.

There is a kind of excess in writing which is 'bad art' not because it is offensive but because it is ineffectual. If Red Riding Hood turned out to be the Wolf herself, or if the Grandmother was busy eating the Wolf when Red Riding Hood arrived, or if the Woodcutters were from the R.S.P.C.A. and insisted that the Wolf should have its liberty, we could accept these innovations as new twists to the story. But if when Red Riding Hood reached the cottage she found the Wolf consuming Grandmother and there was a detailed slaughter-house description of Grandmother's entrails white and wiry and half masticated on the floor, we should reject it because its excessive realism was a lie in relation to the rest of the story.

So with details of sexual relationships, and so with those of mental disturbances. To go too far is to blunder into feeble pornography or scientific case-history, neither of which, as writing, can be anything but mediocre. A lesbian relationship can be conveyed with tenderness, with horror, with pity, with admiration, in almost any way the author likes, but let him try to describe the physical acts or, with his clumsy plodding determination to miss nothing, to follow the relationship to bed and however skilled a writer he may be he will become dull and perhaps silly. So with lunacy, blasphemy, excretion, animalism, sadism and certain kinds of violence—excess of detail or failure to suggest effectively without trundling on drearily into the explicit, makes bad writing. What a poor conventional thing would have been *Heart of Darkness* if Conrad had insisted on telling the reader exactly what Kurtz did among his savages.

It is not restraint that is necessary or that spinsterish kind of restraint called good taste. It is the power to suggest when suggestion is more effective than specification. The power. . . and it is curious that writers who fail in this, who pile on the clumsy stuff that robs their work of effect, are often called 'powerful' writers. Pornography, blasphemy, dirty violence are marks of feebleness, not power, confessions of failure, not triumphant battle-cries against convention.

That is why Nathanael West's two short novels *Miss Lonelyhearts* and *A Cool Million* amount to nothing more than a psychopathic screech. Each is based on a good idea, so good that the very titles are inviting and for once the blurb need only say what the book is about to set the reader on the text like a terrier. '*Miss Lonelyhearts* is a perfectly controlled, bitter comedy about a reporter who is assigned to his newspaper's agony column. At first he treats his job as a joke, but the pain and bewilderment in the letters he receives begin to prey on his mind. When he actually tries to help his correspondents his rewards are madness and death.' The idea is almost too good, like those plots for novels which are for ever discussed in Fleet Street pubs and never written because they can be told in a few words. It is a beauty, a winner, a cinch. It only remains to see what the author makes of it.

On the whole, a mess. He is like an unskilled actor taking a part he has seen played by a competent star. He tries too hard. He is awed by the shocking nature of his subject and he is deter-

mined at all costs to shock his reader. 'You shall *not* be entertained,' he seems to say, 'you shall *not* see a way out, or even
have a moment's material comfort while you're reading me.
No one shall have a drink in my book without going on to
hopeless drunkenness, no one shall show any intelligence without being mad. There shan't be one hour of trivial day-to-day
living in the story, or anyone who wants it. The people who
write to Miss Lonelyhearts are suffering, you understand, and
you've got bloody well to suffer with them.' The result, of
course, is that the reader does not suffer at all, and after
a time loses interest, because he has ceased to believe in
Miss Lonelyhearts and those round him. They are carried to
excess.

It is the book of an amateur, of a man determined at all costs
to attract attention. I know nothing of Nathanael West except
—as I read in this book—that his real name was Nathan Wein-
stein, he was a hotel manager and co-editor of *Contact*, worked
on film scripts and was killed in a car crash before he was forty.
But I am sure he was impatient for recognition and was prepared to go to any lengths as a writer to obtain it. It has come to
him, ironically enough, after his death and in a jumbled way.
His books are curiosities rather than triumphs. He will be
remembered, if at all, as a master, perhaps the master of over-
writing.

Yet in one instance West showed that he had unusual talents.
The letters to Miss Lonelyhearts which he quotes in the book
represent far more than virtuosity. They are indeed shocking,
they achieve what the book as a whole cannot. They are true—
far truer than if they had actually been written by Sick-of-it-all,
Desperate, Broken-hearted and the rest of them. They are so
good that one is angry with the author for wasting them on a
tricksy story of their recipient behaving more or less symboli-
cally, hearing Shrike's far too intelligent and rhetorical jeers,

[*105*]

having some stale love-affairs and finally being shot in a painfully apt and arty ending.

A Cool Million is not even that. A self-conscious satire, it is too clever by half—and too long by half, too. No, this is one of those sudden ephemeral reputations which are bound to flare up in an age when we are all looking for fire.

8

THE ADRIATIC

I was growing tired of the *Trepča* and the silent and remote politeness of the crew. During the two days and a half to Venice I found this exasperating for I had now been almost a month without more human contact than was afforded by odd conversations ashore. Previous passages by cargo boat I had found interesting because I had entered into the life of the ship, heard its daily tittle-tattle, seen something of its workings, been—however briefly and superficially— adopted. Now I was thrown on the resources of reading and writing, not such a bad thing perhaps, but scarcely constituting a holiday.

The saloon intended for passengers I never entered, preferring to remain in the dining saloon where the steward was available. When this was noticed, the crew had little by little adopted the passengers' saloon, playing table-tennis, holding impromptu concerts or sitting in conversation.

'What would happen if I decided to go in there one evening?' I asked Boris.

'I guess they wouldn't come any more,' he said after deep thought.

In each of the Italian ports after Savona Boris had been given a heavy police guard which did not leave him night or day till the ship sailed, for recently a Yugoslav deportee from America had made his escape in Genoa and not been heard of again. Boris bore this invigilation with good humour and it was I who became annoyed when one unshaven policeman carried his enthusiasm to the point of watching over Boris at meals and sat himself in the dining saloon. I was not going to eat under the eyes of the law and told the Chief Steward that either the policeman must go or I must eat elsewhere. Rather sulkily he took himself off but remained in the passage outside, now and then thrusting his head in to see that Boris had not gone through the porthole.

I watched Boris reading one evening, his lips slowly moving in the manner of semi-literates, his whole being concentrated on trying to draw some sense from the printed words.

'The Captain says nothing will happen to me when we get to Yugoslavia. They'll question me, I guess, then let me go to my home.'

'Oh, you've got a home?' I asked because I had thought of him as one of the world's strays.

'I s'pose I have. I haven't written or heard nothing since I left. I'll go and see anyway. Boy, will *they* be surprised to see me when I walk in?'

He grinned, showing his out-turned ape's teeth, powerful and clean but misshapen.

'Why don't you write a story about me?' he asked me once. 'All that's happened to me would make a good story. I'd tell it you. I shouldn't mind.'

'You have told it to me.'

'Not everything though. Did I tell you I had two children in the States with different mothers? Then how I went away to Canada while I was on probation. They was going to let me stay there, then decided they wouldn't. I'd have been all right then. I'd tell you all about that. And what this judge in the Juvenile Court said when they told him I was with this girl. Why don't you write it? You'd make a fortune out of it. All about how I ran away in the first place and lived with those shepherds in Greece. I can still speak a bit of Greek. I worked for a Greek in the States once.'

'What are you going to do now, Boris?'

'I don't know, but sooner later I'm going back to the States. You earn a lot of money there.'

'You don't seem to save much.'

A look of ghoulish cunning came to his face.

'I've got plenty of money over there,' he said. 'Only I had to hide it when they was coming for me. I got it hidden away where no one won't find it. That's what I got to go back for, part from anything else.'

'It may be rather difficult now you've been deported.'

'I can go back in through Canada. I'm going to tell you where that money's hidden to show I trust you. What city, I mean. It's in Denver. Only no one won't find it only me.'

2

I once saw an inscription on the wall of a public urinal which, in six crude and brutal words, gave all the hard meaning that the love-poets of the world had conveyed in thousands of lyric frenzies. At least so I maintained as a young man of undergraduate age in a serio-comic little sermon with which I must have bored my friends. 'No luck,' said the inscription, 'Can't get a . . . ' But you see the idea.

My humour was fatuous and adolescent but I was reminded of its theme by a novel I read coming up the Adriatic called *Butterfield 8* by John O'Hara. Not that there is any lyricism in it—on the contrary, O'Hara never raises his voice to laugh, weep, rave or revel. But here too is a tiny core and a vast mass of sheer garrulousness. The author cannot stop talking about this, that and the other, putting in bits of 'atmosphere', bits of stray characters' stories without point or relevance, bits of dialogue, a long-playing record of relentlessly emphasized triviality.

The fundamental story could have been told in almost as few words as the lavatory inscription. A girl is interfered with, not very seriously, by a dirty old man when she is eleven and seduced by another dirtier but more respectable old man when she is fifteen. The effect on her is to send her to drink and drugs and promiscuity and when she at last falls in love with a married man who is also in love with her she can't take it. She either falls or throws herself (it does not by then much matter which) from the bridge of a ship and is drowned.

There is no reason why this should not make the plot—if there must be one—of a fine novel, but O'Hara seems ashamed of having a plot at all and keeps trying to hide it behind curtains woven in a detailed pattern of half-realized ideas, unintegrated by-plots and unfinished anecdotes. It does not work. The book describes many things in the speakeasy age, an ever-interesting period of American history in which O'Hara is thoroughly at home. and so is never really tedious. But the roundabout slovenly prose becomes irritating, and the steady monotone of the narrative seemed like the ship's engine beating beneath me as I read.

It has energy, that certainly. It reads as though it was dictated at high speed to a brilliant shorthand typist by a man

he portrays so convincingly. A silly question perhaps since Holden only exists as his creation. But this is one of those rare books in which creator and created alike seem to be moved by forces beyond their knowledge, for which the precedent that immediately comes to mind is once more *Hamlet*. We have spent four centuries arguing about Hamlet and it is tempting to say now that we know no more about him than Shakespeare did.

Holden Caulfield is presented as a misfit. He runs away from a school from which he is in any case to be expelled, he spends a week-end in New York behaving in an irresponsible way before his family find him and send him to some unspecified kind of Home in California from which he is to be discharged for a return to a new college. All this is told in a running monologue by Holden, most beautifully written in the racy patois of a rather literary-minded ignorant American seventeen-year-old. (For the brilliance of this form of presentation, incidentally, no praise is too high. An Englishman who has never been in the United States must recognize its authenticity as easily as those who talk like this.) Holden explains why he does everything, and his reasons from his point of view are always valid. He admits to the violence of his prejudices and one cannot help sympathizing with most of them. He dislikes almost everything and everyone generally popular, though he owns that his dislikes are mercurial and his enthusiasms fleeting.

'They are all out of step but our Albert,' and the horrifying fact about this novel is that this is true. The world with which Holden is at odds is the world we know, a world in which failure to conform must always receive its punishment, and success is being like everyone else, only more so. Holden is not wise or articulate enough to know why he hates the guts of his high-class school, why he is the only boy who does not watch the football game of the year, why at times he detests the popular and handsome Stradlater whom everyone adores, or why at other times he likes the unclean and pimply Ackley whom everyone loathes. He recognizes his own varying likes and dislikes and has the courage of them. 'Grand. There's a word I really hate. It's a phony. I could puke every time I hear it.' But he does not recognize his own courage or congratulate himself on his own private resistance movement. If he thinks about it at all he calls the rest of the world phonies and morons, but does not pride himself on being neither. Nor does he realize where this will take him or measure his strength against the massed strength of his enemies. He has no idea that he is going to be rounded up by the psychiatric sheepdogs and made to follow the flock, or else be turned to some hideous fate like 'failure', or genius, or real lunacy, or alcoholism, or perversion, or suicide.

There is little enough room for Holden anywhere in the world but no room at all under the American Way of Life. The strength of Salinger's book is that he shows us this. Slyly or ingenuously, consciously or guided by a half-realized talent, the author appears to be studying an immature overgrown boy, but in fact he is satirizing an age, a nation or mankind.

The magnitude of his achievement is impossible to calculate. I like to think that if I had read this book in 1945 when it first appeared I could have predicted that it would start a whole school of fiction, as it undoubtedly has done. Not only in portraits of adolescents like Clint Williams in James Leo Herlihy's *All Fall Down* or Frankie Addams in *The Member of the Wedding*, or the boy in Sillitoe's *Loneliness of the Long Distance Runner*, but in portraits of pseudo-adolescents or creatures of arrested development, like Keith Waterhouse's *Billy Liar*. This last, in fact, is a comedy English Holden Caulfield, and it is difficult to imagine any of the others having been written before Salinger's book, though it goes without saying that the authors may not have read *The Catcher in the Rye*. To have 'founded a school of writing' has a grandiose sound but means very little compared with writing a good book, and 'schools' have been 'founded' by books of little or no intrinsic significance.

This one, I gather, has not escaped interpretative theorizing and exegesis. Holden Caulfield's simple loathing for the phony has caused his week-end to be seen as Youth's pursuit of Reality, which as he himself would say is crap. Symbolism has been found in this straightforward narrative and Salinger himself has become a sort of cult. Perhaps his later books justify this—there is certainly nothing in *The Catcher in the Rye* more than a noble piece of fiction, satirical, compassionate, moving and gorgeously written. Who wants more, anyway?

4

I turned for contrast, hoping for rude and blatant humour or creepy effects, to two books, *Kiss Kiss* by Roald Dahl and *The Bishop's Jaegers* by Thorne Smith, titles which promised to demand very little mental effort from the reader.

The first was the greatest disappointment. When one reads, as a quotation from a review—'If you like Tom Lehrer's songs and Charles Addams's cartoons, you are going to rave about Roald Dahl's *Kiss Kiss*', one is entitled, surely, to something more than warmed-up Marion Crawford stories with trick endings, written in the manner of the railway bookstall magazines of thirty years ago. I do like Tom Lehrer's songs and Addams's cartoons, but I do not see the connection. These tales plod along and the contrived uncanniness which is meant to make them macabre and sophisticated gives them no more than a clumsy touch of the old-fashioned ghost story. In spite of the

[115]

pearance of most of them in *The New Yorker* and a critic's description of them as 'diabolically ingenious' I am out in the cold again for I can find nothing here but mediocrity.

The collection starts with a landlady who has poisoned her previous tenants and keeps them embalmed in the attic. Then twenty-five pages are given to one of those science-fiction experiments by which a man's brain is kept alive to amuse his wife in the long winter evenings. This is twenty pages, at least, too many. (Even the title of this one, 'William and Mary' was used by Max Beerbohm with far too much effect for its reissue here.) The story that follows, though hoary, is told with a certain engaging nonchalance—a woman letting her irritating husband die in an empty house because the lift sticks between floors as she departs for a holiday. 'Parson's Pleasure', the next story, was done better by H. A. Vachell in *Quinney's* and O. Henry might have written 'Mrs Bixby and the Colonel's Coat' with more subtlety. Then there is one of those stories which turn out, on the last page, to be written in a lunatic asylum, and a reincarnation tale (Liszt returning as a cat) for which Saki would have used half the words with twice the effect. Finally a poaching farce which does not come off.

I expected even less of *The Bishop's Jaegers*. What could follow that title but the corniest gags? Yet I might say, in the manner of Roald Dahl's reviewer, if you like Bob Hope's merry chit-chat and P. G. Wodehouse's good-natured fun you will—perhaps not *rave* about, but certainly enjoy this book. All the characters talk like Bob Hope all the time and all the situations are like Wodehouse's, though their occasional smirking impropriety is the author's own.

But even in 1934 when this book was published and its author died, nudism, bell-voiced bishops, unconscious male victims of designing females, baffled magistrates and obese ex-models must have been a little *vieux jeu* as comedy topics, and

[*116*]

today they seem painfully dated. When, I wonder, shall we find a humorist of our own times who speaks in a natural voice and is content to be funny?

5

The three most boring topics of conversation are, in this order, (i) The Strange Dream I had Last Night. (ii) The Phenomenal Intelligence of My Dog and how he shows it. (iii) The Extraordinary Capabilities of my Car and how I drive it. All, it will be seen, forms of exhibitionism, attempts to hold an audience without the necessary narrative power or suitable material.

Moreover, anyone who tells a long detailed story of a dream, full of supporting detail and humorous dialogue, is a liar. Dreams are only memorable when they continue, as it were, into consciousness, so that their conclusions are not dreamt at all but experienced by the waking mind. Even then only inconsequential scraps remain.

There is something else against retailing dreams nowadays. They give psychologists the most extraordinary theories about you and nothing will convince these psychologists, professional or amateur, that they have not acquired startling insight into your past, your nature, your sub-conscious mind and what not, even if you have deliberately invented the dream to mislead them. If you say you dreamed about grasshoppers they reply knowingly: 'Yes. Your father had an Oedipus complex.' Give them that one about falling off a cliff and never reaching the bottom and they smile and say something you don't want to hear about the libido. I have often wanted to try telling a psychologist I dreamed I was falling *up* a cliff and never reached the

[*117*]

top, but I've always funked it. It might mean I'm certifiable.

I did once tell one, in a man-to-man conversation (for I've never been in a consulting room), the perfectly true and to me rather interesting fact that I once had a whole series of dreams about the late Queen Mary.

The psychologist nodded at once, in the way they do.

'Quite ordinary,' he said.

'I beg your pardon. It was nothing of the sort. I had never consciously thought about Queen Mary. I have never taken more than the most casual interest in the doings of the Royal Family. I could not escape seeing occasional pictures in the press of Queen Mary during her life-time but if I thought about them at all, which I don't remember doing, it was of a dignified lady doing her duty. How can my dreaming of her, not once but a dozen times, have been ordinary?'

The psychologist smiled. Like all the psychologists I have known he smoked a pipe and now drew from it complacently.

'Compensation,' he explained. 'Thousands of people who believed themselves insufficiently important to their parents in childhood seek compensation in dreams in which they are adopted by members of the Royal Family. It's not a pheno-menon, it's a commonplace.'

'What about the Royal Family?' I asked. 'Have they no say in the matter?'

'They don't know—unless they read Freud.'

'If what you say is true it seems rather hard on them, being dreamed about in thousands of homes every night.'

The psychologist gave his nothing-can-shock-me smile.

'One of the burdens of royalty,' he said, and left it at that.

All this is leading up craftily to a dream I had on the night before we reached Venice. But the reader need have no fear. It is not a long circumstantial story but a snatch of recollection and dialogue.

I was back at my preparatory school. That was not unusual —I often visit my various schools in dreams. Only this time, though still apparently taken for a pupil, I was grown up. I was facing the terror of the school, the cane-wielding headmaster, who stood six foot four and was tremblingly referred to as Mr B. Nothing unusual there, either. I had often faced him in childhood and in dreams. But this time instead of pointing to the arm of a chair with his cane, he was gazing at me with sickening benevolence.

'How old are you now?' he asked kindly.

'Twenty-four.'

'You're rather old for the school.'

I found myself struggling through tears to speak the truth.

'I'm over fifty,' I shouted.

Then I must have been on the point of waking for I was acquiring some of the diplomacy which would come with the return of consciousness and grinned feverishly.

'I've been under you all these years,' I said.

Now I was awake. But I had spoken the truth. Who having known a Mr B in childhood, with his cutting strokes of cane or speech, ceases to be under him for the rest of his life? Down there in his caverns of the sub-conscious Mr B reigns supreme.

9

VENICE

Venice was under snow.

I have known the city in spring when only in its people is there an air of reawakening; its grey house-fronts with little vegetation remaining old and impassive. I have seen it in summer, too, when the new wine of its youth ferments along the Lido. In autumn it is most tragic, a sad echoing place of slow movement and dripping stucco. But the city I saw from the deck of the *Trepča* as she passed slowly through the Canale San Marco towards her moorings was a ghost city rising from the water, white under a grey sky.

The lagoon was still and the ship's engine scarcely seemed to disturb the hush of the early morning. We passed between San Giorgio and San Marco, scarcely two hundred yards from the piazzetta which was as yet untrodden. The *campanile* and the two huge columns in the square (trophies brought home triumphantly by a Doge eight centuries ago) were capped with snow and St Mark's itself was domed and blanketed with white, a most curious and beautiful vision.

We passed the piazza too swiftly. Already the first black figures were moving across its white expanse and I realized that before the ship berthed and I had time to return, the virgin surface would be broken and muddy, and the white miracle extinguished. But by the chance of being on a ship passing at dawn after a snowfall, itself no common event in Venice, I had seen something which made the time of my winter cruise well chosen. The piazza, though it cannot be altogether cheapened by sentimental photographs and films, by shoddy marble models and by pigeon-feeding tourists, has become in popular memory an attractive playground, essential in a European tour, a sunlit square over which the café tables spread while cameras click unremittingly. Here was Venice unpopulated, undefiled, 'so quiet, so bereft of all but her loveliness, that we might well doubt' (said Ruskin) 'as we watched her faint reflection in the mirage of the lagoon, which was the City, which the Shadow'.

I knew Venice a little better than most visitors, a good deal less than the artists and writers who have fed their talents here. As we went on our way through the Guidecca Canal and passing the Jesuits' church made for the basin, and as I returned by waterbus up the Grand Canal, it seemed flatly incredible to me that more than twenty years had passed since I was in Venice. So well remembered, so entirely unchanged was each landmark, each separate loveliness, that my last stay here might have been unbroken by a war and two decades of vivid living and the ups and downs of my forties and fifties. I passed the Scalzi church, spendidly Baroque, the Ca'd'Ora with its gold and colours gleaming through the snow, the Rialto bridge, the long string of Gothic palaces lining the canal, as though I were meeting old friends after a few days of separation. I remembered the Doge's Palace so well that I hesitated to revisit it. In my

[121]

mind the 'giants' staircase' with its colossal statues of Neptune
and Mars rose immensely from the court and I could still see
something of Tintoretto's 'Bacchus and Ariadne', and hear the
guide saying it was the largest oil-painting in the world. I remembered the sense of intrusion I had felt in the Doge's
Palace, as though I were impertinently examining someone
else's possessions, as though the Doge himself had just left it
and would return.

I decided that for this first day at least, until the snow had
thawed or lost its brightness, I would visit no interior but be
satisfied with the embalmed and muffled city which was
strange and yet familiar to me.

2

I had not realized how ancient were the foundations of
Venice, or that St Mark's was built before the end of the
eleventh century. Architecture is indeed the most precocious of
the arts and some of its most sophisticated triumphs came
before men had learned to paint on canvas, to print, or to
compose more than plainsong. It is to me very wonderful that
the world's most beautiful churches were planned by men of
simple vision and built by primitives. It is not wonderful at all
that pinchbeck techniques and ferro-concrete can produce
nothing except mass effects, or that architecture, becoming a
domestic science in the eighteenth century, should have failed
us wholly in the nineteenth and twentieth.

Ruskin groaned at the later and more florid beauties of
Venice in purple passages, like an Old Testament prophet
crying doom. He cursed the Renaissance in Renaissance prose.
But Venice, secure from invasion by modern transport,

unmolested by the motorcar, undisturbed by all but river
traffic, has turned the tables on him. He writes:

And now I wish that the reader, before I bring him into St
Mark's Place, would imagine himself for a little time in a quiet
English cathedral town, and walk with me to the west front of
its cathedral. Let us go together up the more retired street, at the
end of which we can see the pinnacles of one of the towers, and
then through the low grey gateway, with its battlemented top
and small latticed window in the centre, into the inner private-
looking road or close, where nothing goes in but the carts of the
tradesmen who supply the bishop and the chapter, and where
there are little shaven grass-plots, fenced in by neat rails, before
old-fashioned groups of somewhat diminutive and excessively
trim houses, with little oriel and bay windows jutting out here
and there, and deep wooden cornices and eaves painted cream
colour and white, and small porches to their doors in the shape
of cockle-shells, or little, crooked, thick, indescribable wooden
gables warped a little on one side; and so forward till we come
to larger houses, also old-fashioned, but of red brick, and with
gardens behind them, and fruit walls, which show here and
there, among the nectarines, the vestiges of an old cloister arch
or shaft, and looking in front on the cathedral square itself,
laid out in rigid divisions of smooth grass and gravel walk, yet
not uncheerful, especially on the sunny side where the canons'
children are walking with their nursery-maids. And so, taking
care not to tread on the grass, we will go along the straight
walk to the west front.

With this quiet and idyllic picture he contrasts the approach
to St Mark's, 'resonant with cries of itinerant salesmen, a shriek
at their beginning and dying away in a kind of brazen ring-
ing'. There are lamps in the shops burning before pictures of
the Virgin and in a shop marked *Vendita Frittole e Liquori* the
Virgin is enthroned beside a tallow candle on a back shelf,
while at the regular wine-shop the Madonna is in great glory
above ten or a dozen large red casks. We pass the 'frightful

I   [123]

façade of San Moise', and notice with disapproval 'the modern-
izing of the shops' and 'the mingling of the lower Venetian
populace with groups of English and Austrians'.

We find that:

Round the whole square in front of the church there is
almost a continuous line of cafés, where the idle Venetians of
the middle classes lounge, and read empty journals; in its centre
the Austrian bands play during the time of vespers, their martial
music jarring with the organ notes,—the march drowning the
miserere, and the sullen crowd thickening round them,—a
crowd, which, if it had its will, would stiletto every soldier that
pipes to it. And in the recesses of the porches, all day long,
knots of men of the lowest classes, unemployed and listless, lie
basking in the sun like wizards; and unregarded children,—
every heavy glance of their young eyes full of desperation and
stony depravity, and their throats hoarse with cursing,—gamble,
and fight, and snarl, and sleep, hour after hour, clashing their
bruised centesimi upon the marble ledges of the church porch.

How was poor Ruskin to foresee that his 'little shaven grass-
plots' before an English cathedral would become littered
with ice-cream cartons thrown from motor-coaches, that
car parks would run to the very walls of the church, that the
west doorway would be crowded with motor-borne holiday-
makers who 'might as well have a look inside now we're here',
that the sound of the bells, if there is anyone who knows how
to ring them, would be drowned by the starting of motor-
cycles, the screech of klaxons? While here in Venice, pro-
tected by nature, and one might think by man's foresight,
from the devastation brought by wheeled traffic, St Mark's,
one of the most visited churches in the world, stands undisturbed among the pedestrian hordes of summer.

Why have we never learned to do what nature has done for
Venice? Since we cannot build anything worth while why do

we not preserve what we have inherited? It did not need much imagination sixty years ago to see what was coming to a town like Oxford and it could have been made something like a walled city without walls to protect it against the corrosive tide. Imagine its colleges enshrined and unmolested by the builder or the motorist, one city at least which could not be entered except on foot. Its splendour and charm would have been increased tenfold, as are those of Venice, by the thudding engines outside its gates, the din and vulgarity of an ever-increasing traffic jam in the roads encircling it. It is too late now for it is the very hub of England's traffic and motor-trade, and its colleges and churches are jostled by shops and cinemas with fronts more 'frightful' than San Moise presented to Ruskin.

So one of the great and distinguishing charms of Venice is a negative one—there is no road traffic. That the canals have grown motorized and the gondola more (though not entirely) a fad for tourists is true but it does not affect that divine negation, that arcadian absence of the noise and tempo of motor-traffic. To be able to walk the streets in one's own time unchivvied by cycles, unthreatened by cars, is more than something quaint, old-fashioned and unique. It is to know what cities were and could be again, perhaps will be again if man is ever progressive enough to halt or at least restrain the mischief that science has brought.

Not that Venice, relieved of the din of engines, is a quiet city. On the contrary its people seem anxious to fill the silence with their voices, with bells and music and shouts of laughter. But if you listen, it is as though a buzzing in your ears had stopped, as indeed it has. It is not the silence of night-time elsewhere, deep but always under the threat of disturbance. It is a street-noise heard nowhere else, the street-noise of other centuries.

[125]

The city has almost as many literary associations for the English as for the Italians themselves, from Shakespeare's *Merchant* to Byron's and later Hood's seizure of the name—the Bridge of Sighs, Shelley's invocation, Wordsworth's ecomium and many more. But during this winter visit the writer who came to mind was poor paranoiac Frederick Rolfe, starving through three successive winters here, writing pornographic letters at so much a time to titillate the appetite of a homosexual debauchee, cadging, blackmailing, threatening suicide, swimming and sailing dangerously, sleeping on open stairways, yet unable to leave Venice because he loved her and could face no future but this. In his bad, eccentric, bitter book *The Desire and Pursuit of the Whole* his mad passion for the place and his familiarity with its underworld is almost shocking. I could see *him* here in the snow, with his sparse hair dyed red, with his 'tatters and slippers and no pocket handkerchief', walking by with what he himself believed was 'his cruel and pitiless and altogether abominably self-possessed serenity of gait and carriage'. Or, during a sudden period of prosperity earned by embezzling money from a well-wisher, 'on the canals with a new boat and (a privilege usually reserved for royalty) four gondoliers'. It was just half a century since Rolfe's death, and little had changed in Venice but the cut of men's clothes and women's fashions, and the wares in the shops round the piazza. Something in this city makes all books about it topical.

Foreigners receive no attention from the passing Venetian who has seen them in their hundreds of thousands, in every kind of garb, with every eccentricity of manner, talking every tongue, striving to mark their own distinctions now that they are all brought to the common level of pedestrianism. The

Venetian knows them best in summer, photographing one another among the pigeons, but he is not surprised to see them in winter, hurrying as I did through the snow.

To the visual glories of his own city he is, of course, indifferent and this roused Ruskin's disapproval. 'You may walk from sunrise to sunset,' he claimed rhetorically, 'to and fro, before the gateway of St Mark's, and you will not see an eye lifted to it, nor a countenance brightened by it.' What on earth did he expect? Do Londoners gape at St Paul's or have their 'countenances brightened' by the Abbey? Even paradise must grow commonplace at last to its inhabitants.

Besides, that morning, perhaps because the snow made everything unfamiliar, eyes *were* raised to St Mark's and the campanile and to those two columns bearing one the lion of Venice, the other the city's first patron saint, St Theodore, with his foot on a crocodile.

Of all I saw that day, and in the two days that followed, it is not the curious nor the aesthetic that is chiefly lively in my recollection now, but the opulence of the ancient city, which is ubiquitous and overpowering. The Venetians were merchant adventurers and they brought home the spoils of trade, barter, or plain robbery from the East and West, to adorn their churches and palaces. They were tycoons and could employ the greatest artists and architects, the most skilled craftsmen, to build and beautify. They were also men of excellent if lavish taste and though the results of their centuries of creation and collection are exuberant, even at times ostentatious, they are never uninspired or pretentious.

Well though I remembered the interiors of Venice nothing in my recollection matched the reality for its richness both of design and materials, the luxuriousness, the flagrant prodigality of it all. The buildings were extravagant enough in what

[*127*]

Ruskin called the Grotesque Renaissance style; their interiors, with Titian's riotously fertile masterpieces and Tintoretto's voluptuous frescoes, with their almost oppressive wealth of carving and gold, their mosaics and the florid splendour of their capitals and sarcophagi, are like the Judaic dream of paradise, which may well have been their model. St Mark's with its mosaics, its marbles, porphyries and alabaster, its tessellated work of marble and glass, its Pala d'oro, that triumph of the goldsmith with its encrusted gems and enamel run into gold plates—it is almost, but never quite, too much.

I made no planned itinerary, only taking a glance or two, as it were, undiscriminating and brief, at the inexhaustible gorgeousness. I had no time for intelligent sightseeing which, for me, is almost a contradiction in terms. I might have done better to select two or three paintings and study them but, again for me, that would have been a priggish and unnatural occupation. Each of us must take what he can from a few days in this city and I took a mindful of opulent beauty.

4

I made the Danieli my headquarters, not only because after such luxurious sightseeing I wanted a superlatively good hotel, but also since on two of my previous visits to Venice I had stayed here so that among hotels it was my natural choice. It seemed to have changed little and had a pleasantly out-of-season spaciousness and ease about it, its porter's desk free from visitors inquiring eagerly where they might hire a gondola or purchase Venetian glass and beads.

The food, from its great kitchens, probably half-staffed in winter, was fresh, well-cooked, excellently served but un-inspired hotel food and I enjoyed it daily, preferring to come here to an atmosphere of copiousness, civility and comfort than to look for gastronomic treasures elsewhere.

To reach it I had to make my way with difficulty through half a mile of snowbound dockland, dangerous stairways over railway lines with ice-covered steps, through a number of cold streets to the Piazza Roma, from which I got the water-bus to the waterfront station of San Marco. That run between the churches and palaces of the Grand Canal, under three bridges, the Scalzi, the Rialto and the Accademia out into the lagoon, is a memorable experience at any time, in these frosty mornings it was stimulating and delightful. There is, as they say, a book in it, if it has not already been done. A trifle obvious, perhaps— *Through the Grand Canal, From Scalzi to Zaccaria*, something of the sort, full of lore and history, architectural appreciation, lavish descriptions of interiors not usually seen, all illustrated with etchings by Whistler and James McBey. But perhaps the day of such pleasant Edwardian travel books has gone and the modern reader demands not archaeological but zoological specimens for his entertainment.

The arcades round the Piazza San Marco, those 'arches charged with goodly sculpture and fluted shafts of delicate stone', the Procuratie Vecchie and the Procuratie Nuove, I ex-plored not only in search of books but because the square itself grew slushy as the snow thawed and was trodden, and the arcade made a sheltered walking place like ornate and shop-lined cloisters. Most of the shops were closed that month and for books I was conducted by a page-boy from the Danieli to a street of little antiquarian bookshops where even the Penguins were second-hand. But I left Venice with a fresh supply.

5

On what turned out to be (though I did not know it) our last evening in port I stayed on board. I can find plenty of excuses for it now, the difficult and perilous walk through the docks, the fact that there was no opera or theatre, the cold, but I still must recognize it as a defeat. I remember how forty years earlier, on my way to South America, I bounded ashore at each Spanish port, remaining till the gangway was about to be drawn up, and how shocked and compassionate I was because one passenger, an elderly man, did not trouble to take the launch ashore having seen this port before. If I am ever so old, I thought, that I don't want to see *every* foreign town and as often as possible, it will be time to die. As for missing a night in Venice . . . So while I had all the logic on my side in staying aboard it was not without compunction, even a touch of shame, that I did so.

One excuse for remaining at home I had heard from others but never had cause to use it myself. There was 'a book I wanted to read'. A particular book about which I felt a special curiosity, *Cider with Rosie* by Laurie Lee.

There had been a lot of critical gush about this book and H. E. Bates had called it a prose poem, a ridiculously paradoxical term, which, if it has any meaning at all, is damning to a book whether in prose or verse. There had been too much excited '*have* you read? . . .' a form of enthusiasm usually, I find, worked up over the most slick and ephemeral achievements. Also, I may have felt some small jealous prejudice because it had phenomenal success four years after a book of mine, which covered some of the same ground, had sold my usual modest couple of thousand copies. Moreover the author had a tiresomely alliterative name which, for some reason 'put me off'. One way and another I was not ready for its merits.

At first I thought I was right in my scepticism. For the first chapter or so Laurie Lee seems to be trying to do that impossible thing—give a child's-eye view of the world. It has been attempted before, like a dog's or a cat's-eye view, and has always failed, as it always must. However potent the imagination and acute the memory, no man can see only as a child and record only a child's perception, and if he could the result would be tautological and tedious. On the very first page, recording the experience of himself at three years old, left alone on a garden bank for a moment, Laurie Lee says too much or too little. But even here he says it beautifully with an exact yet allusive prose, a confident clarity, and none of that self-conscious searching for new, original, startling terminology which sickens me in the work of second-rate modern poets. Within twenty pages I was wholly captivated.

The tot's-eye manner is dropped and though the sensations and impressions of childhood are faultlessly conveyed there is nothing artificial in the manner of conveying them. They are lived in memory, not just recalled.

No one has done this particular thing so skilfully, or no one in this century. The only echo, very faint and very rare, is of Kenneth Grahame, yet I somehow doubt whether Laurie Lee had read either *Dream Days* or *The Golden Age*. His book is so completely his own that he might be wholly unliterary or badly read. Not that there is anything primitive about his work—it is polished and rich. But he has that rare thing, a style, and it is his own style, not a compounded one, not deliberately trained by example or knowingly adapted from others. It is flexible and economical and used with legerdemain. He can raise a storm in a few lines and bring the buzz and heat of a summer day into your brain with a couple of sentences. He can touch your very palate with the taste of coarse country food and fill your nostrils with the scents of a stuffy interior or of

[*131*]

harvest-time. He can do anything he likes with words while he is within the limits he has set himself—the re-creation of a vanished epoch and a home life of three or four decades ago. Whether he can do more than that, whether this splendid instrument which he plays so well is capable of rendering more ambitious themes, cannot of course be guessed. But part of the triumph of this book is that here it is used to the full and not forced beyond its capacity.

Perhaps only a fellow-writer or a seasoned critic or at any rate a man who is in one way or another wholly dedicated to letters can know the ecstasy—no lesser word is needed—of reading prose like this. It is like sitting at the wheel of a new Rolls-Royce after years of chuffing about in old cheap motor-cars. It is like owning a perfectly proportioned Georgian house after living on a modern building estate. Or, more fairly, because it is not merely smooth and inoffensive, it is like going to Kew after dibbing in a back garden. With all those metaphors I mean that one has that blessed confidence in the author that so rarely comes nowadays, one *knows* he will have the only word, turn of phrase, figure of speech. One ceases to be sur-prised, ceases to notice this perfection and gives oneself up blissfully to the theme.

Here was my only disappointment—that there was a theme, or perhaps I should say a wrenching of the theme to an alien and not quite natural purpose. Laurie Lee re-creates a certain life at a certain time and does it supremely well. Why then force some special significance on it? Every decade is the ending of one epoch and the beginning of another. Why try to con-vince us that this one, 1917 to 1927 approximately, was more so than many others? If he is saying that it saw the end of the horse and the take-over by the petrol-engine he is a long way out. The horse was doomed and the motor-car an everyday vehicle ten years earlier. Nothing in a Cotswold village such as he paints had changed much twenty years later, when I lived in one which still had its squire and almost everything else described in this book.

This attempt to give his book an external significance seems false and modish, but it is the only thing which is either. The rest is sheer joy. The people live, not as characters in a novel or as characters in history. They live here and now in these pages. Dead or alive they continue to live and will continue. For they are not characters but beings, and their blood is not printer's ink.

6

The Chief Steward was doubtful, on our last morning at Venice, about the ship's sailing time, but thought I should return from the city by two o'clock. I wandered rather aimlessly through the streets which were now cleared of snow and dawdled in an attractive small market noticing the dearness of food and the good humour of vendors and customers, realizing regretfully that my days on the canals and in the alleys were over, at least for a season or two.

When I returned to the ship I found much bustle and excitement. Orders had come from Rijeka and we were sailing at once.

10

RIJEKA

The lights of Venice from the lagoon traced in brilliant strings the outlines of St Mark's and its piazza and not till late in the evening had the last shimmer from the islands quite faded. We should cross the Gulf of Venice before morning and tomorrow come to Rijeka.

During the voyage I had read most of three translated French novels and I finished the most famous of them, Gabriel Chevallier's *Clochemerle*, that evening, an uncomfortable book, like a smell of drains. This and *The Green Mare* by Marcel Aymé are both of a type now recognized and—it would seem—sought after, a gamut of rustic fornication, graphically delineated bosoms and buttocks, lascivious glares from every male in the village from the mayor to the twelve-year-old schoolboy, all described with a resolute attempt at Rabelaisianism which does not succeed because it is self-conscious. Honest ribaldry I find healthy, refreshing and often hilarious; it is when it is dishonest, smirking and arty that it nauseates. I felt at the end of these that if I had to read another passage about the joys

[*134*]

and humours of urination, the infidelities of farmers with saucy servant girls, the incontinence of kindly old curés, or willing skirt-lifting by impossibly simple country wenches, I should be driven to spew. More so if such passages were punctuated by bickerings about mortgages, savings, inheritances, expectations, and lawsuits, or weary details about the crops or small shop-keeping.

Once is enough. I could just about take *Clochemerle* though I should have thought its bogus earthiness would have bored most Frenchmen. It is written in a winking, nudging, have-you-heard-this-one style which means to be bluff and coarse but which I find affected and smutty. But it does move, and in a peasant-in-books way its people live and have their eventful being. They are caricatures, but animated ones, like figures in a Disney cartoon. The action is clockwork, too, and instead of rattling up to a comic climax ends in such bathos as a naked madwoman appearing in a church pulpit.

It is only fair to say that Marcel Aymé's *La Jument Verte* (*The Green Mare*) was published three years before *Clochemerle*. Both authors are Burgundians and Aymé is the younger man. His book has an unpleasant quality of sophistication. It is as though he were saying—'I'm a clever chap and I *could* be writing about people of intellect and distinction. You can see by the way I treat them that I don't *need* to write about peasants. But we'll have a laugh together at such simpletons. Wait till you hear it. You'll scream!'

Well, if I do, it is with irritation. Bosoms and buttocks again, marriages and mortgages, cunning and ... countrified manners—it's all a big yawn to me. And what's the point of it? If the author could bring it off he would only be doing what has been done better a thousand times. Even his approach is not novel and he has to drag in his green mare as a dashing stroke of surrealism.

[135]

I suppose it is a mode and French fiction will leave it all behind if it has not done so already. It must have been a gift to the French tourist industry, though. The British and Americans already have a curious way of speaking of continental countrypeople as 'peasants' while their own are 'land-workers' or 'villagers'. Seeing these 'peasants' presented by Messrs Chevallier, Aymé and the rest, must add a great deal to a family motoring-holiday in France. They no longer appear as the tired and inscrutable field-workers they once were to both French and foreign observers, but as satyrs in a dream fantasy of perpetual priapics. The women, poor souls, seen hurrying home with their shopping-baskets, are no longer busy housewives. Busy they may be, but with intrigue, infidelity or incest. The men, fresh from work, are going home to domestic orgies or hurrying over their meal to keep their appointments in the ever-convenient hayfields. The young children can scarcely wait to drop their school satchels at home before they begin their nightly revels. Every roadside spinney is rustling with copulation and everyone envies someone else's cornfield or vine-trees, everyone is scheming to get someone's will altered in his favour, or to marry his son to the butcher's daughter who has two thousand francs more than the baker's. Excretionary functions are given the maximum publicity and every childbirth is a scandal. It is a very odd world indeed that the *Clochemerle*-reader sees from the window of his GB car and it must add a lot of variety to his holiday. It is to be hoped he does not suppose that he himself can enter into the spirit of the thing for then his disillusionment might be complete—and violent.

The world of François Mauriac's *The Unknown Sea* is a little more distinguished, both socially and as literature, and it is to be noted that as a Penguin it is bound in grey, to denote a 'modern classic' rather than orange which means a mere book.

It takes place in the Bordeaux district instead of Burgundy and lovers of claret may find something symbolic in this. The people concerned are, with a few exceptions, a cut above the vintners and innkeepers of *Clochemerle*, they are lawyers and moneyed or dismoneyed people in a big city and there are even a few scenes in Paris. But here, too, is this monotonous obsession with inheritances, dowries, mortgages, wills and greedy ambitions which are shown to condition the lives of a number of young people of two families. Why do French writers seem determined to convince us that no one who lives outside Paris thinks of anything but money or the power that money brings? Perhaps some of Françoise Sagan's success comes from the fact that—so far as I remember—she never gives it any significance in her novels.

But there is this to be said about *The Unknown Sea*—it is very evidently not the author's masterpiece. I have read nothing else of his so I do not know how far I am showing my ignorance. But I do know that this is the book of an author who can write far better, who is not 'all out', as it were. There are passages which suggest a reserve of power, and passages which seem written almost absent-mindedly as if by a man who must get this finished before he tackles something really big. One feels one is with a writer of shrewdness and clear perceptions.

2

The approach to Rijeka is a spectacular one through a land-locked fjord of snowy mountains. It was a glorious morning and although I was becoming accustomed to the beauty of sunlight on white peaks, it seemed more dramatic here, with the water translucent and still as the water of a lake and the ship cutting it with scarcely a ripple. Except for the engine there was silence, not placid or benevolent, but eerie, tenuous, waiting to be shattered by some explosion which never came.

Boris had become apprehensive and nervous as he approached interrogation and perhaps arrest, and some of his disquiet must have communicated itself to me for I felt none of the peace of the scene around us. It was radiantly beautiful, and if it lacked reality and the easy green virtue of an English landscape, it had an awe-inspiring reality of its own, like a Turner painting.

A mist like a heat mist—though the air remained icily cold—hung round the coast, and from it Rijeka slowly emerged. It is not a majestic city, or even a picturesque one, but any township seen from the sea acquires some touch of radiance and nobility and this one, in the circle of its foothills, looked pleasant and inviting. Sixteen years ago, I knew, it had been the Italian port of Fiume—one of those cities that has changed hands, and changed its name more than once in the last century.

3

For the crew Rijeka was the end of a voyage. The *Trepča* would remain here for a fortnight and then go to the East while I found my way home on another ship. There was some particular though still reticent good-will shown to me that morning. After all I had been more than a month aboard and had been seen and greeted every day. It was as though they wanted to show that there was no ill-feeling and did so by shaking hands and saying goodbye and speaking a few words of

English, making me understand that unsociability had been forced on them. The stewards put my luggage on a waiting taxi and there were a few shy handwaves as I drove away.

There was no fuss at the dock gates—a glance at my passport, a nod and I was in communist country for the first time and if not exactly behind the Iron Curtain, a rusty piece of drapery in any case, at least in a country of stern anti-capitalist principles. The taxi was noisy and decrepit, the driver noisy and beefy, so with din and incomprehensible shouts to me from the front seat, and some laughter, we came to the Hotel Bonavia.

This, like every other hotel, bar or shop in the country was state-owned but like many of them seemed anxious that it should not be too depressingly obvious to visitors from less orderly Western states. It is not too obvious, at a glance. The hall-porters in the conventional uniform of the *concierge* who are also the booking-clerks say with adequate civility what rooms are vacant at what price. Someone brings in one's baggage. One finds one's room small and rather bare but, with bathroom, it costs exactly one pound a night. One comes down for a drink in the bar which has no bar-stools but twenty tables with fairly comfortable chairs. A good Scotch whisky is served. One lunches well, looked after by conscientious waiters. This, one decides, might be any modest hotel anywhere.

Only slowly does one begin to feel the deathly impersonality of it, and the cause of that is difficult to trace. This ranks as a first-category hotel, so furnishings, of uniform quality throughout the country presumably, are the best one will see anywhere and are grimly sufficient, no more. The row of bottles behind the bar will be reproduced behind every first-category bar. The food conforms precisely to a certain standard. The waiters are trained like soldiers to their duties. And after a time it begins to seem that the customers conform to standard, too. They have adequate drab-coloured clothes such as one sees at men's shops in the town. The women are allowed more variety in their dress but this too follows a pattern. Chairs, tables, crockery, glasses, all of a certain fairly high quality. There is not a touch of fantasy in the hotel.

Yet human nature breaks out. One hall porter is more helpful and more humorous than another, one waiter quicker and more gloomy. And though the customers wear standard suits there are no less oddities of face and behaviour among them than in any other crowd of people.

The hotel consists on the ground floor of two large rooms of equal size, a dining-room and a lounge-bar. Behind them is a small room with a few chairs in it and a vestibule where the staff keep their overcoats. They come in looking exactly like the customers in the lounge, dressed in thick suits and overcoats, and don the uniform of their calling. A lift goes to the barrack-like landings with the rows of numbered doors. Everyone is rigidly polite, helpful, cheerful, even welcoming. In a sense, the hotel is well run and everything has its advertised price. But how one longs for the occasional incivility, even the occasional overcharge or small internal crisis, in a French provincial hotel where the *patron* and *madame* are visibly in command.

It is not a drab or an unhappy atmosphere. On the contrary there is raucous laughter in the bar and usually a few meaty tarts sitting around—distinguishable even here from respectable townsfolk. There is plenty to drink and money passes freely. A general, in uniform, one of the highest paid men in the state, entertains a party of friends. An occasional near-drunk lurches by. Greetings are loud and hearty. There is a heavily festive air in the lounge at night. Yet conformity, orthodoxy, standardization hang over it like a cloud.

[*140*]

4

Of what value, I wondered, to me or anyone else, could be my observation of Yugoslavia when I had only a week or two to pass and could not speak the language. In England we are well informed about the country by statisticians, writers, journalists. We know its history, ancient and modern, its agricultural production, its trade figures, and when there are events which make news they are fully reported in our press. The only thing we do not know, unless we have been there, is what it is like.

By that I mean, I suppose, how it compares with our own in matters of everyday life. We may know how much is earned by people in each category of worker, and how it is spent. We may know how communism, as an economic principle, has been made to work. But we don't know how it feels, how we should like it, whether we could be happy here except on a spoon-fed holiday at Dubrovnik. These things I began to discover within an hour of arriving, for they were what interested me. I wanted no details of Tito's Cabinet or its aims, no airy theorizing, no sensational eye-witness accounts of notable events. I am a working bourgeois with bourgeois hopes and fears and I wanted to know how I should find life here. That, at least, was my angle of observation.

I walked, that afternoon, through the main shopping street of the town and found it a somewhat daunting experience. State-owned shops with state-paid assistants and state-supplied goods do not encourage window-shopping. Two of them sold handicrafts and these were more cheerful for their goods are made by individual craftsmen who not only work independently and for themselves but may employ—as I learned later— up to seven workers. The wood-carving was quite good and there were some hand-woven materials and carpets, all at prices which were high by local standards.

I went to a café which was frankly depressing—a railway buffet sort of place crowded with men in second-grade clothes as the lounge at the Bonavia was crowded with those in first grade. It was open, like our own pubs, for fixed hours, and once again uniformed waiters served standard drinks at bare uniform tables.

Perhaps what emphasized the standardization of the place was its architecture, the large ornate ugly buildings built in the time of Austro-Hungarian occupation. Many of these were being pulled down and replaced by equally ugly modern utilitarian blocks, one of which, of sixteen storeys, was known as Express Corner and seemed to arouse civic pride, for when I asked where to find a certain office an English-speaking Yugoslav told me it was in 'the sky-scraper building'. But everywhere are remains of the nineteenth century or of the Italian past of the town. My narrow room at the hotel had once been part of a much larger one as the great creaking window showed. There were ornate street-lamps in some streets which modern lighting had not yet reached and in the back room of one shop still hung that symbol of its age, a hideous glass chandelier. Italian was not talked in the streets but it was understood everywhere and, one suspected, could be heard in many homes. These vestiges of the past are being shuffled off as quickly as possible, for Rijeka, chief port of the new Yugoslavia, wants to forget the empire and d'Annunzio and Italy and become a spruce and modern city and port for a great merchant fleet. The process is no doubt expedient, perhaps necessary, and will make for the greater good of the greater number, or something of the sort. But it is not a very cheerful thing to notice on a grey winter afternoon in a town of muffled-up severe-looking citizens serving, willingly or not, an alien ideology.

[142]

Thinking there might be something of that past to buy I asked if there was an *antiquat* and was directed to the state-owned pawnshop. Perhaps the past was treasured in secret, or perhaps the manager refused pledges of more than a certain age, for the goods on offer were of the present, shoddy manufactured things of no interest or value.

A more serious deficiency for me was that there were no cigars to be found in Rijeka. Since abandoning cigarettes fifteen years ago I have formed the habit of smoking a dozen mild cigars or cheroots each day, finding this healthier and more economical than the paper-bound wisps of tobacco of which I was smoking sixty a day. Healthier, but just as habit-forming, and difficult to relinquish. Without cigars I am a half-man, a ravening werewolf pursuing tobacco. I have been in no country, in those fifteen years, where cigars, smokable though sometimes unfragrant, were not obtainable, however high the tariff wall. Spain, Morocco, Germany, France all had their particular offering—even in Great Britain *panatellas* are to be bought at disproportionate prices. But here was nothing, not even smuggled Havanas or those dry little Dutch whiffs one finds almost everywhere. By great good luck I had a few Ramon Allones which I was keeping for special occasions and with these, and a dozen little cigars presented to me by a Dutch skipper met at the Bonavia, I had to get through my time in Yugoslavia, a tiresome disability.

5

At night the hotel grew crowded and it was difficult to find a seat in the lounge. The customers were mostly from the town and hung their overcoats on pegs behind them while they

sat for hours over their beer or local brandy. The air grew
smoky and thick and there was a good deal of noise. This was all
of gaiety or entertainment that higher salary earners could find
unless they went to the cinema. Later there was a sad little
cabaret in the town but the lounge of the Bonavia was the
nightly resort of many citizens whose faces I came to know.
They seemed unnaturally tall after other Mediterraneans. Are
the Yugoslavs an unusually tall and powerful race? They appeared so to one coming from Morocco, Spain and Italy.

But the food was good. The Yugoslavs are proud of their
national cookery and have restaurants which advertise it—
'Restaurant avec Cuisine National.' It is Balkan in spirit,
Turkish by descent, but none the worse for that. On my first
day I had a scampi soup better than I had tasted in Italy, a dish
called Djuvedje which was local—pork with rice, tomatoes,
green peppers—and a rich pastella.

I was happy enough in Rijeka. Everyone was good-
humoured, everyone tried to understand and to oblige. Those
who came from a penurious past were pleased with their
prosperity and there was no sign of embitterment among those
whose prosperity had been reduced to fit the pattern. It was
not a sullen grey town, such as one imagines East Berlin, or
furtive and fearful like the towns of Stalin's Russia. But it
certainly was not gay.

11

LJUBLJANA

I planned to go to Ljubljana to look for something which could no longer exist, but which was so vividly in my mind that I felt compelled to lay its ghost.

A quarter of a century earlier, almost to the day, or in less high-sounding terms in February 1938, I had come to Ljubljana, also on an impossible quest and in highly incongruous circumstances. Two years before the outbreak of war, when writers and journalists were flocking to the Continent to interview Stalin, Hitler, Mussolini, or one of their senior minions, and coming back with material for books or articles on 'Will there be a War?' I hit on the idea of travelling round Europe to interview the man in the street on the same subject. A cynic might have objected that such a person's views had no longer the smallest significance, but I found a publisher who liked the idea and advanced me a couple of hundred pounds —sufficient at the time—to make the journey. With this I purchased a Morris Commercial which had done twelve years' service as a bus on the Welsh roads and persuaded two brothers, sons of a travelling circus proprietor, not only to convert the bus to the purpose of a living-waggon but to spend the winter travelling with me. We had passed through Belgium, Holland, Germany, Czecho-Slovakia, Austria and Hungary and if I did not learn much from 'The Man in Europe Street' (the title of the book I afterwards published) I had a riotously good time. The old bus rattled on through snowdrifts and over difficult roads which had become almost impossible when we entered Yugoslavia.

One grey afternoon when snow threatened but did not fall we came to Ljubljana, the capital of Slovenia, which should have been the very place for material such as I was supposed to be seeking but which had other, very different attractions. We were accustomed to the pitiful cheapness of everything in eastern Europe and particularly in Hungary and Yugoslavia, but nothing prepared us for the Stari Trg.

This was a street in the poorer part of the town which consisted entirely of little second-hand and antique shops kept by Jews. They were stocked with a confused miscellany of objects, fine old furniture, painted wood-carvings, carpets, silver, pottery, cast-off clothing, chandeliers, paintings, fabrics, glass, old boots, skates, toilet ware and books. At the first shop I stopped idly and saw a fine carved statue of St Teresa of Avila, three feet high, probably of the seventeenth century and having its original colour and gilt. I asked the price and was told in dinars a price which hastily translated turned out to be seven and sixpence. Incredulous, I inquired about a pair of altar candle-sticks in beaten silver of about the same height and found they would cost me fifteen shillings. Then I lost my head a little. I went on to other shops and found fine Balkan rugs at half a sovereign each, a painted tray with a brilliant landscape for less than a pound, an eighteenth-century mahogany card-table for thirty shillings, and so on. It was a collector's dream.

[*146*]

If I had possessed a hundred pounds and means of transport and had kept what I found I should be a rich man today.

But I hadn't. I had less than twenty pounds in dinars and I spent it all. The living-waggon had to be rearranged to hold my purchases under the bed. Round me still as I write are some of the things I found in that buyer's bedlam. Until war broke out I dreamed of raising the capital to go back to Ljubljana to exhaust the whole market. And here I was within a hundred and fifty miles of it.

Of course the street could no longer be there. Those tumble-down houses would have been swept away by the new broom of communism and any of their occupants who had survived the war would have been transferred to more useful callings. Shops were state-owned and such little private concerns had long since been obliterated. Yet it was so clearly in my mind, that occasion when I had for once been able to afford beautiful and curious things, that I had to go back and see for myself what had replaced it. A sentimental journey if ever there was one.

So on Sunday morning I took the train from Rijeka.

2

Rather to my surprise there were first- and second-class carriages on the train, but the first were bare and had narrow seats covered with artificial leather which smelt of oil, while the second were not much better than cattle-trucks.

At first we encircled the bay at sea level passing the resort of Opatija on the coast, then began to climb. For an hour or two, while the snowbound slopes faced the south, they sparkled in sunlight and the isolated villages with the mosque-like spires of eastern Europe looked cheerful enough in spite of the long miles of bare snow which separated them. This was unbroken save for the occasional track of a wild animal—fox or hare, I supposed, though the solitude and distance suggested, to my hyperbolical mind, a wolf. At village stops in the hills a few passengers alighted and I could see well-trodden tracks to the church doors, but at Postojnska there was a long wait, time to get a cup of hot coffee laced with brandy. Here were advertised the remarkable grottoes and I read uninvidiously that I could travel for twenty-one kilometres underground by electric railway to the habitat of *Proteus Anguinus*, that little eel-like salamander, sometimes called from its pink colour the human fish.

From here the railway passed into a sunless region where the snow lost its glitter and the sky was leaden. There were fewer villages and the landscape grew Russian and grim, as though one were crossing the tundras or making a journey on the Trans-Siberian railway. This was the country of the Slovenes, as different from the sunny coastal belt with its pretty resorts as it is from Scandinavia or Switzerland, desolate, impoverished, sparsely populated at any time and on this February morning chill and forbidding.

Nor did Ljubljana, when we reached it, seem a very sparkling or welcoming city. It was now one o'clock and the population must have been indoors eating their Sunday meal for near the station there was scarcely a passer-by and I waited half an hour while a taxi was telephoned for. Even the centre of the town, under thick dirty snow, saw little movement, but the Slon Hotel, when I reached it, was bright with electricity.

'Slon' means 'elephant' and the hotel must have been named, like many of our inns, like the Elephant and Castle, from some heraldic design. Perhaps the kingdom of Illyria, whose

[*148*]

capital Ljubljana was during its brief existence (1816–49) had
an elephant in its crest. The reference can scarcely be to Jason,
the legendary founder of the city, or the Emperor Augustus,
the historical one. Whatever its nominal origin, the Slon Hotel
has few marks of an ancient hostelry. Great bare rooms and
passages, adequately warmed, furnished with bright new chairs
and tables and bright new fabrics from state-owned factories,
give it a 'modern' look such as one sees in coloured advertisements of furniture stores. On the fourth floor of long landings,
like the landings of a prison brightly painted, I was given a
bare room with bath at thirty shillings a night, complete with
one comfortable bed, one chair, one table, one mirror and one
carpet, all clean, fresh and wholly impersonal.

The restaurant was immense and here again the appointments were adequate but without character. The waiters also.
What is it, I asked at intervals in Yugoslavia, that is lacking
here? Perhaps it is *chance*—nothing is left to chance, nothing
exists by chance, all is orderly and there is no extraneous
detail, no relic of a former regime.

3

But there are always miracles. I had just finished eating
some excellent smoked trout when there entered, impatiently
using a walking stick, a little white-haired merry-faced woman
who went straight to her table and after giving a detailed order
to the waiter in the Slovene language began to read a novel
by Dorothy L. Sayers while she awaited her food.

I asked about her. Her name was Mrs Copeland, the waiter
told me, she was ninety-one years old and had recently broken
her leg in a mountaineering accident. Recently? Well, a few

months ago. Mrs Copeland was a great Alpinist. She was known by everyone in Slovenia, Croatia and Dalmatia. She lived in this hotel.

As soon as she had finished eating I went and introduced myself and was given a vigorous and talkative welcome. Yes, it was so annoying about her leg. It was taking a long time to set. Yes, she quite liked Dorothy L. Sayers's books. Did I want to borrow any? She had plenty in her room *and* the *New Statesman* of last week or the week before. If I liked to come up with her I could see what she had. She was quite used to lending books to English people. They seemed to find her out. She was sometimes considered a sort of British Consul here. Quite unofficial, of course. People came to her because she spoke the language. She had lived here on and off for forty years.

I went up to her room and found it dominated by two pairs of skis, a discarded crutch and the paraphernalia of mountaineering, besides a great quantity of books in English and many framed photographs.

'This was my father,' she said, handing me a picture of a magnificently whiskered Victorian. 'He was Astronomer Royal of Scotland.' (I think that was the title.) 'He was a fine man. Only recently I was told that modern atomic science owes a great deal to his researches. I have a son too, only he's really rather too old for me, if you know what I mean.'

Garrulity was her only symptom of old age. She could not stop talking. Perhaps her isolated life here in this Slovene city made her glad of an English audience, but she was scarcely less loquacious in Slovenish, I was to find. I wanted desperately to ask her about the Stari Trg and the antique shops of twenty-five years ago, realizing that she may have been in the town then. But I could not manage to insert even the briefest inquiry.

'I do a good deal of translation into Slovenish, Children's

books, chiefly. I can show you some in bookshops—I don't keep them here. And I'm writing my memoirs. I have a publisher interested in that. You see I was the first person to be arrested when the Germans came.'

'Mrs Copeland, I wonder . . .'

'Yes, they arrested me straight away, but I wasn't badly treated. Oh, no. There is a kind of brotherhood among Alpinists and the German officer who arrested me was one. He was really very nice. He knew of my climbing, you see. Then they gave me the choice of prison in Germany or Italy. I chose Italy, of course.'

'I wanted to ask you . . .'

'I came back here in 1949 and have been here ever since. I know it so well, you see, and I think I'm fairly well known in this country after living here all these years. I was in Florence during the war and stayed there for a time. But I like these mountains. You wanted to borrow some books, didn't you?'

'As a matter of fact . . .'

'Just choose what you want. Here's the *New Statesman*. I've cut out the correspondence. Something annoyed me in it.'

'Is there an antique shop in the town?' I shouted suddenly.

It worked. I had time to follow it with a description of the shops I had found before the war, the little street, the Jewish dealers, the unbelievable bargains.

Mrs Copeland swept all this brusquely aside.

'Still there,' she said. 'Still there. In the Stari Trg. I took some people there the other day.'

'But they can't be. All those shops. It's twenty-five years ago. The war . . .'

'Yes. Still there. I'll take you tomorrow. That pile of paper is my memoirs. A publisher wants them but he has asked me to cut them down. He thinks they ought to be about half the

[*151*]

present length. I don't know whether I shall do it or not. Found something to read? That's good.'

Further questions would clearly bring me no nearer to a resolution of doubt. Mrs Copeland's airy 'still there' could not be taken seriously, yet suggested that something remained. Had it not been so pitilessly cold and dark in the streets I would have investigated that night. As it was I felt no temptation to leave the hotel.

4

I was down in the entrance hall early next morning, but not so early as Mrs Copeland whom I found talking with the hall-porters, greeting passers-by (almost indiscriminately, it seemed), a busy woman who would have been positively bustling if she had not been lamed by a mountaineering fall in her ninety-first year.

I said I would order a taxi.

'Taxi?' she said tartly. 'What do you want a taxi for? It's only about half a mile. We'll walk.'

Pavements and roads outside were a death-trap, the slush having frozen hard during the night. I pointed this out.

'Nonsense. It's not far.'

At this point one of the porters asked me if I had ordered a taxi and with relief I lied affirmatively. Mrs Copeland was not pleased.

I did not remember Ljubljana well enough to decide now how much it had been improved and enlarged since the coming of communism but it seemed quite an imposing city as we drove down. Busy, too; the Sunday sparseness of yesterday had given way to bustling crowds.

'It's just down here,' said Mrs Copeland after a fairly long and circuitous drive. 'You see, you didn't need a taxi.'

There was no sign of the street I remembered, no squalor, no little crowded shops, no eager faces in the doorways. The taxi stopped at a large shop called Dom and we got out.

'Here you are,' said Mrs Copeland pointing at the windows of Dom with her stick. 'Isn't this what you wanted?'

It was a handicrafts shop, bigger and better than the one in Rijeka but full of basket-ware and modern pottery.

I tried to explain.

'Oh, antiques,' said Mrs Copeland without interest, 'that's farther down.'

It was. No little shops each cheaper than the last. No profusion of objects at negligible prices. No keen little salesmen. But one solid, well-arranged antique shop owned by the state and managed by a party official.

So my journey was not altogether in vain. I started to examine things and ask prices contentedly and with some relief. I was living out the tail-end of a private fantasy which had been behind my mind for twenty-five years. I was so completely absorbed that for some time I forgot Mrs Copeland.

She, however, was not to be forgotten. She had taken a seat at the end of the shop and for a while was content to talk loudly in Slovenish to the assistants, then turned on me.

'What are you looking for?' she asked. 'What on earth do you want these things for?'

I offered to take her home and return to look about me. No, she would wait. I could take as long as I liked. Did I want this? Or that? Why didn't I examine the pottery? That was Slovenian, she knew. She did not much like the smell of my cigar. Look—those were all carpets over there. She would ask the manager to show them to me if I liked. But perhaps I did not want a carpet?

I was almost recognizing objects from that long-ago visit. It was not impossible that some of them had survived and found their way at last to the state *antiquat*. Surely I had seen that Holy Child before with his glass dolls' eyes? I wanted, more than anything to be left alone.

But Mrs Copeland had been extraordinarily kind in bringing me here. I tried to remember my manners.

What about that sword? she asked. If she were going to buy anything that was the sort of thing she would buy. There were some books down there. Had I noticed them? No, no. She did not mind waiting. Only that cigar. And hadn't I decided anything yet?

Oh, dear. I had come all the way from Rijeka, perhaps in a sense all the way through the Mediterranean, for this and I was not to be allowed to enjoy it. I felt petulant and childish. 'Really,' I said, 'I am sure it would be best if I didn't bother you any more, Mrs Copeland. *Please* let me take you back to the hotel and return here later.'

But why? I wasn't going to be here much longer, was I? I had seen all there was to see? She did not mind waiting a few minutes longer. Hadn't I looked at that before? She thought we should visit the cathedral.

In the end I desperately purchased two geometrically patterned rugs in strong good colours and a Macedonian primitive ikon. But before doing so I completed a thorough tour of the shop. There would be no more dreams of lost chances in the years ahead.

5

The walk back was not a happy experience. To trudge for what seemed a mile over frozen snow, each step taken with caution, beside a chirping nonagenarian who refused any aid or attention, was something of a nightmare, particularly as my obligation to Mrs Copeland was great. She hobbled along surefootedly but at each miniature glissade on the pavement I thought she would slide and crash, rebreaking the leg which was taking so annoyingly long to set.

Moreover she insisted on visiting the cathedral whose outline rose ahead of us.

'It's supposed to be one of the finest examples of Baroque in eastern Europe,' she said. 'Its frescoes are famous.'

We entered a solid Renaissance building whose ceiling was smothered with mediocre paintwork. Surely nothing is uglier than a bad fresco.

Mrs Copeland watched me narrowly. It was not any denominational pride which was at stake—she had told me firmly she was not a Catholic—but her anxiety as a citizen of Ljubljana of many years' standing that this feature of the town should be admired.

'Wonderful, isn't it?' she said. 'I don't like that kind of thing myself but it is said to be the finest example of Baroque . . .'

'Hideous,' I said firmly, and with not much exaggeration.

'You *think* so? But I'm told it is unique.'

'It may be. It's hideous,' I said. 'Do let's get out of here.'

Mrs Copeland, looking rather baffled, made for the door. I was failing badly as a visitor in need of her aid. But she did not withhold her monologue as we walked to a bookshop where she had a number of assistants to address in their own language while I looked through the Penguins. At last, prattling with undiminished gusto, she entered the Slon and hurried across to the desk for a chat with the hall-porter. I thanked her for her kindness which I thought remarkable, but she

L

had not much attention to spare from a Slovene disputa-
tion. Magnificent, indefatigable, age-free. I watched her
chatter her way to the lift and wondered whether Lady
Hester Stanhope herself was more loquacious or more brave
in exile.

12

THE *IVAN MAŽURANIĆ*

The return journey to Rijeka was more eventful than the outward one for I discovered by chance that part of the train in which I was sitting was bound for Trieste and Rome. At Postjana I moved to the Rijeka part of the train only to find no first-class carriages—a trivial misfortune elsewhere but in Yugoslavia meaning a penitential wooden bench in a bare truck for the rest of the journey.

This was not without interest, however. Most of the passengers were neatly clad and fairly prosperous-looking artisans but sprawling over a bench not far from me was a creature who seemed to belie all the provisions of a welfare state. He was perhaps in his forties but the unshaven face, horribly lined and dissipated, could have been of an older man. The greying hair was thick and matted and he had a heavy unkempt moustache. He wore a tattered khaki shirt and cotton trousers in spite of the cold and his sockless feet were in broken shoes.

He was drunk. Snores like wild animal sounds shook him and the people around smiled pityingly at this. Then he started scratching himself, pulling out his shirt to do so and exposing a dirty torso, at which a couple of women moved farther away. Such wretchedness and degradation seemed to belong to the underworld of Dostoievski or Gogol, not to this tidy industrious country where the least-skilled work was adequately paid and no one wanted the means of life. A destitute dipsomaniac? A mild lunatic? A born tramp untameable to decent standards? Certainly wreckage.

But he had a surprise for me. The train jolted to a halt and the man awoke, sat bolt upright and stared about him with dull bloodshot eyes. Then in English, with an intonation that suggested a public school and university education, he said clearly—'Where the devil are we? Haven't we got to Rijeka yet? Blast these slow trains.'

I would have tried to learn something of him but at that moment two guards appeared to put him off the train for having no ticket. He pulled on a tattered overcoat and went without a murmur, evidently accustomed to such expulsions.

'A train vagrant,' explained the man next to me in English, but could tell me no more.

2

In Rijeka I made several acquaintances, among them a young English engineer who came to the country on business several times a year and had married a Yugoslav girl now in England. He was both knowledgeable and informative about many aspects of Yugoslavian life, A staunch admirer of Tito, he could yet call Djijlas 'the uncrowned king of Macedonia' and say he was a remarkable man who had to be curbed.

'In a country like this,' said the engineer, 'you can allow opposition to individuals, but not to the system.'

Well, yes. Put like that. Wasn't it true of our own regime? But I did not want to talk politics, rather of their effect in the lives of the people. The engineer was optimistic. The 'have-nots' were happy, of course, and even the former 'haves' were reconciled. There was plenty of incentive to skilled workers— if they could earn more by having their own business they were entitled to do so. Perhaps business was hardly the word, for what was rigidly forbidden everywhere was buying and selling for profit. If you could make a better suit than the next man you could charge more for your work but you could not deal in ready-made clothes. Nor could you keep a shop, or advertise.

'Don't you notice the absence of advertisements?' asked the engineer. 'Most visitors do.'

But there is advertisement of a kind, particularly of travel and entertainment. What is absent is competition in advertisement and how refreshing that is. No roadside hoardings each higher than the last obliterating the view, no searching through periodicals for a rivulet of text between the contorted faces of photographers' models, no vociferous interruptions of radio and television services.

The personal experience of my acquaintance had been from the first reassuring. He had been struck, as I had, by the natural kindness and honesty of the people and after he had learned the language had made friends everywhere. I asked him if he did not find something drab and toneless about it all.

'You have been in two rather drab towns, after all; Rijeka and Ljubljana in winter are scarcely frivolous places.'

It was interesting to hear this intelligent and rather conventional Englishman with an upper middle-class background defending in practice a regime which in theory he must have

[159]

abhorred. Defending it, that is, for these people and for this country, unable to accept it for his own.

That day's *Times* had given details of the first case in Russia in which a group who had made a fortune out of food adulteration had been sentenced to death. The engineer made no protest when I said that if there must be a death penalty this was the most intelligent use for it, but the idea, lightly developed, led to flippancy as we visualized English caterers being hanged in rows and our cooks being dragged to the scaffold.

I dined with him and several English-speaking Yugoslavs and their wives. Highly paid executives with comfortable flats, they showed no reticence in discussing, and in certain small ways criticizing, the regime, just as Spaniards criticize theirs. In speaking English they had a far larger vocabulary than most English people and made subtle use of it, producing some surprising but forceful effects, like Conrad in his early novels.

We ate Dalmatian smoked ham—delicious but no better than Spanish—and sea-bream cleverly cooked. We talked of the food we ate and other foods and Yugoslav cookery which at its best is superb, a compromise, like so much else here, between Western and Eastern, with all the originality and stark contrasts of the Balkans and Near East, and some of the delicacy and directness of Italy. There would seem to me no more pleasing or more unexpected aspect of communism in Yugoslavia than that under it the national cookery and the quality of food have improved, not only in the homes of the workers but in public restaurants and hotels. When I said that Yugoslav cherry brandy seemed to me the finest obtainable and—if not a contradiction in terms—a great liqueur, I was told that the finest of all came from Maraska, a district adjoining Zadar (which the Italians called Zara). I was told moreover that the people of the country share with all other Slavs a fondness for hard liquor and thrive on it. This seemed good news to me, for not till East and West can drink together will there be any security of peace.

3

The other friend I made was a young Yugoslav who being employed as a shipping clerk spoke several languages. He had done his conscripted service in the navy and showed me with some pride a photograph of himself in uniform taken a few years earlier.

He took me to his home and I was interested to see his circumstances. On a clerk's salary he could afford a bachelor flat of two rooms, which he rented furnished, in a rambling last-century house. Most curious was that the furniture, and even the curtains and upholstery, were pre-war. No sign here of bright mass-manufactured chairs and tables—the bed was of mahogany and there was a faded Victorian air in the place. So the new regime had not yet reached all the interiors, I thought, and wondered whether there are still lace curtains and antimacassars in Moscow.

On the wall was an extraordinary picture. It was not dated but must have been printed in the first decade of this century, a coloured oleograph depicting the queens of all the countries in Europe crowned and in full regalia. There were no less than eighteen of them, staring haughtily ahead, with sashes and decorations, with immovable-seeming coiffures, with jewelled collars and glaring eyes. Our own was Alexandra who shared the honours of the central position with the Empress of Germany and the Tsarina. I realized the fact that fifty years ago there were only two republics in Europe, France and Switzerland, whereas now there remain no more than seven kingdoms.

But was this elaborate piece of iconology in any worse taste than the ubiquitous portraits of Tito, Franco, Kruschev and even de Gaulle which stare down at us today?

4

At the offices of the Yugoslav Line I received a telegram summoning me urgently home and at the same time heard that the ship on which I was due to sail, the *Ivan Mažuranić*, had bunkered in Gibraltar on her way into the Mediterranean and consequently would not call there on her way to England. I asked when the next ship would be sailing for Gibraltar and was told there would be none for three weeks.

This was thoroughly disturbing and I set myself, as long ago I had learned from my father, to get my own way against seemingly impossible odds. The official in charge of the passenger office was patient and understanding and at him I volleyed my arguments. The Line's agent in Tangier had told me that there would be no difficulty about my return, ships leaving each week for Gibraltar. I had trusted this and expected fulfilment of a promise. I could not fly and there was no other way of return. Veering slightly I called for sympathy. I was being called home on account of illness, for my son (as I called my Indian secretary with only a touch of euphemism) was seriously ill, as this cablegram would show. Surely the Jugolinija was not going to be so unfeeling as to ignore this?

But what could they do? asked the official.

They could drop me at Gibraltar, as originally arranged, I pointed out gently.

The official at once dismissed this as out of the question and absurd. Politely but as though he could not even consider the suggestion he asked how they could stop at Gibraltar to drop one passenger? Did I know what it meant to bring a ship into a port?

I had a fairly good idea, but I now adopted an air of childish ignorance of all such maritime details. I *had* to get home. I had been assured that the *Ivan Mažuranić* would call at Gibraltar. After all, it had to pass within a mile or two of the Rock.

I sensed the beginning of something that could not yet be called weakening in his manner as he answered with assumed indignation.

Stop a cargo boat at a port to drop one passenger? Unheard of. Had I not read the conditions of passage? This was a *freighter*. There were considerations of cargo. Time. Distance. Obligations to agents. It was made clear in the company's literature that passengers could only be carried on this understanding. To suggest that a ship should actually call at a port . . . the time . . . the expense . . . the delay.

Still, I said, and kept my place in his best armchair.

Couldn't I go by train to Marseille? he suggested desperately. There was a frequent service of boats from Marseille to Tangier.

Impossible. I had my return ticket on the Yugoslav Line. This was a health trip. I had made the most rigorous inquiries before booking. I had been told on arrival that the *Ivan Mažuranić* would call at Gibraltar.

The official and I recognized an impasse and solemnly regarded one another for a full half-minute.

'Well, I could ask the head of the passenger service,' he said. 'But I cannot hold out any hope. To make a special call! Such a thing has never been suggested.'

He left me to return after ten minutes with his superior officer, and to him I once again put my case, pleading for justice, fulfilment of obligation, sympathy and assistance at the same time. The superior officer heard me out but the situation was too much for him.

'I don't see how we *can*,' he smiled. 'You see these are cargo ships. . .'

I tried a new line of attack which I could see had no immediate success. I was a writer. I wrote for newspapers as well as books. I was going to write about this voyage. How could I recommend the Yugoslav Line when it failed in its obligations?

'But there was no obligation,' said the senior official.

I played my last card. With an air of having been driven to it, I spoke importantly.

'Then,' I said, 'I must ask for an interview with. . .' What should I call him? 'With the General Director of the Yugoslav Line.'

'With?'

'Impossible!'

'He is not available, I fear.'

I continued to sit as though nothing could remove me from that chair till a solution had been found.

'Perhaps,' I suggested after a while, 'perhaps you could see him on my behalf? I am sure if it was explained to him. . .'

The two officials looked as though they thought me mad. Perhaps they did. But they left the room together and were gone for twenty minutes. Whom they interviewed I shall never know. When they returned they were beaming.

'The *Ivan Mazuranić* will call at Gibraltar!' said the senior official, as though the triumph was his alone.

But his junior felt he must save his face, or that of the Jugolinija.

'It has been found,' he said, 'that a few cases of cigarettes have been brought on here by mistake. These can be returned to Gibraltar by the *Ivan Mažuranić*, so you will be able to disembark.'

[*164*]

I thanked them heartily and to everyone's relief at last vacated my seat.

5

The ship was named after the Croatian nationalist poet Ivan Mažuranić (1814–90) and his portrait, with grand Dundreary whiskers, hung in the lounge with that of Tito. The ship was smaller than the *Trepča* but newer and better appointed; the food was better, too. I was delighted to find that I should have two travelling companions—a North Country solicitor and his attractive wife. As there would be no call between Rijeka and Gibraltar, but five days of rather rough passage, it was good to find that both liked conversation as much as I do and both talked well.

13

AT SEA

I had kept only two books for this passage. I had read both of them before but for different reasons wanted to read them again—D. H. Lawrence's *Lady Chatterley's Lover* and Joseph Conrad's *Nostromo*. I was driven by curiosity to the first for I could not see how the rather silly book I remembered could possibly have caused such a bother; the second I would read as I read all Conrad every five years or so.

When we were all very young I met Allen Lane, not then Sir Allen Lane the founder and chairman of Penguin Books, but a young publisher in his father's office at the Bodley Head. His firm was about to bring out the first collection of Peter Arno's matchless cartoons and a party had been arranged in celebration of this, but Arno himself, at the last moment, was unable to come. Young Lane amused himself and us by proposing—though not with any serious intent—that an American should be found at the bar of the Savoy of approximately the right age who would be willing to impersonate the cartoonist, maintaining that it was the sort of thing Arno himself would approve. It does not sound very funny now, but Allen Lane, having just come from a wedding reception, brought a champagne flippancy with him and discussed the dress, manner and make-up of his bogus artist, who of course was never produced.

When I remember that afternoon I wonder whether the present, doubtless sober-minded and judicious, head of Penguin Books was not indulging his own secret humour in the matter of *Lady Chatterley's Lover* and pulling the legs of the whole British judiciary by including this piece of juvenile smut in his lists, thus forcing that ridiculous prosecution. If so, he was supremely successful. Learned counsel held forth, expert witnesses crowded forward, a learned judge summed up and a solemn jury debated—all over a volume of schoolboy *graffita*. If one of the defence witnesses had said that the book should not be suppressed because it was too feeble, too ill-written and too superficial to influence anyone at all, even a moronic teenager, the case would have collapsed. But God became involved in the witnesses' testimony, and Lawrence's high intentions and noble character were upheld, and an Anglican bishop rushed in where angels, one would have thought, would scarcely care to tread, and the whole dreary farce was reported by the world's press as if to say 'What *will* the English get up to next?'

None of this was incredible or even difficult to understand. Outbreaks of salacious puritanism are not rare and we are a dirty-minded race who enjoy parading such things in the law courts and the press. The rest of the world has come to expect from us from time to time the publicized prosecution of authors and publishers, or the pietistic castigation of a titled divorcee or famous homosexual. That we had been hoist with our own petard and forced for consistency's sake to prosecute the publisher of such innocuous nonsense as *Lady Chatterley's Lover* need not have surprised anyone.

Yet there was one aspect of it which could not be so easily

or so cynically dismissed—Rebecca West had given evidence for the defence, Rebecca West of the cool judgment and the lively critical mind, whom no one in his senses could suspect of publicity-seeking, or self-persuasion, or any kind of dishonesty. It was the recollection of her unaccountable presence in the witness-box which had persuaded me to buy the book and keep it for the homeward trip, which made me examine it now with a determination to find in it something more than I remembered from my long-ago reading of it.

2

When I had finished the first sniggering class-conscious pages I remembered that Rebecca West had known D. H. Lawrence and over the years had defended him several times, though not too blindly to call one of his books 'plum-silly' and I realized that to understand the issues in the Lady Chatterley case one must recall something of Lawrence himself and his writings.

That class-consciousness, for instance, was an integral thing. H. G. Wells started with it, guyed it, made good novels of it and threw it off with insouciance, so that in his later books he could write of the classless world of the successful, which he inhabited, without attitudinizing. Lawrence never achieved this and throughout his life wrote of doings above-stairs as one who hated and jeered at the 'upper classes', never seeing the inhabitants of the big houses he had gazed at in boyhood as simply people like his own friends. This must have come from his mother, an ex-schoolteacher who despised her miner husband and his calling, who entertained the minister from the local Bethel and drove her son onward and upward through the Band of Hope and Christian Endeavour to be a pupil teacher and a high-collared young man, superior to others in her street. Lawrence went onward and upward to be a famous writer, but he could not lose his conscious or subconscious belief in a world he could never enter, a world he could only hate. He was not a rebel, politically or ethically. He made no effort to destroy that world or to change his own. He simply hated it venomously and spent his life creating fantasy substitutes for it, ideal communities in which he could be, not the little boy sent to the back door with a message, but a king enthroned among his followers.

At its meanest and vulgarest his class-consciousness informs the whole of *Lady Chatterley's Lover*. On the very first page one of Lawrence's blatant redundancies is significant—'They returned, Clifford and Constance, to his home, Wragby Hall, the family "seat". His father had died, Clifford was now a baronet, Sir Clifford, and Constance was Lady Chatterley.' Clifford had become 'a first lieutenant in a smart regiment so he could mock at everything more becomingly in uniform. Clifford Chatterley was more upper-class than Connie. Connie was well-to-do intelligentsia, but he was aristocracy. Not the big sort but still *it*. His father was a baronet, and his mother had been a viscount's daughter'.

With more defiance than truth, one feels, Lawrence shows that the miners, *his* people, remained unimpressed by this. 'There was no communication between Wragby Hall and Tevershall village, none. No caps were touched, no curtseys bobbed. The colliers merely stared; the tradesmen lifted their caps to Connie as to an acquaintance, and nodded awkwardly to Clifford; that was all.' Then there is Miss Chatterley 'with her aristocratic thin face' and Clifford's 'aristocratic relations', such as Lady Bennerley, 'a thin woman of sixty, with a red nose, a widow, and still something of a *grand dame*. She belonged to one of the best families and had the character to carry it off'.

[*169*]

This aspect of the book, the class aspect, with which Lawrence is much concerned, is done with a corny obviousness that is more embarrassing to the reader than any details of copulation. It is all an old-fashioned melodrama, the hall, the village, the erring wife of a baronet, the servants who know too much, even the postman who hears voices in the bedroom. It leads up to Lawrence's grand revenge on Clifford for being a baronet (or on T. P. Barber, J.P., for having ordered Lawrence off his ground as a young man) when Clifford hears the truth about Connie and Mellors. 'His face grew yellow and his eyes bulged with disaster as he glared at her.' 'He was silent like a beast in a trap.' ' "That scum! That bumptious lout! That miserable cad! And carrying on with him all the time, while you were here and he was one of my servants!" ' He does not actually shout 'never darken my doors again' but asks instead—'Is there any end to the beastly lowness of women!'

Lawrence's revenge on Clifford (or Barber) is thus complete, and if this is to take too personal a view of the man and his work, it must be remembered that he never drew a character except from life, that for every named figure in each of his books there was a living counterpart and many of Lawrence's delineations were acts of revenge or malice. I have not done the kind of research which would tell me whether or not in fact Lawrence was remembering T. P. Barber, the 'young squire' of his village, when he created Clifford, but it is the sort of thing he did all his writing life with sometimes disastrous results.

3

Most writers are paranoiacs; a few have the good manners to conceal it. Lawrence could not, and paranoia runs through his life like a bugle accompaniment. At first it was a secret from all but such devotees as Jessie Chambers but as the books were published and there was applause to seize on, and blame to resent with haughty disdain, the familiar symptoms break out. A bad review becomes an act of blasphemy, a brush with authority a sort of crucifixion and the only hope is to create Rananim, the place where Lorenzo can be worshipped in peace. 'The critics really hate me,' Lawrence exulted in a letter to Amy Lowell, and he was crying 'persecution'! long before any public hostility was shown to him. His reviews, in fact, were much like any other writer's, great or small, more concerned with showing the critic's perspicacity and smart phraseology than making a true assessment of the book. He had good, bad and indifferent reviews, as who does not, but the bad and indifferent ones made him a Prometheus.

When in 1915 *The Rainbow* was seized by the police, though as Gerald Gould said in the *New Statesman*, 'the most improper thing about it is the punctuation', Lawrence was almost triumphant in his martyrdom, and when defenders came forward and questions were asked in the House, he may well have thought it worth the price, since only a thousand copies had been printed and he had received an advance on the royalties of these. But a greater trial was being prepared for him in which he could see himself as a messianic figure, an outcast whose genius aroused fury, a god wounded by the brutal hostility of mankind. Spending the war years in Cornwall with his German wife he had the not uncommon experience of being suspected as a spy and expelled from a prohibited area. A moment's detached reflection would have told him that this, in the circumstances and at the time, was inevitable and that he was fortunate in being quietly warned to go elsewhere. But no; he cried anguish and expiation and as his wife said 'he sat there as if he had been killed... He had always believed so in everything—

M

society, love, friends. This was one of his serious deaths in belief'.

Perhaps the martyrdom of a medical examination was even more painful to his self-esteem for he was being treated like other men, like all other men of military age. The idea was unendurable to him, and his account of the ordeal (in *Kangaroo*) recalls the later writings of Frederick Rolfe. 'The slight lifting of his nose, like a dog's disgust, brought even the judgment-table to silence: even the puppy doctors.' He would never be touched again. 'Because they had handled his private parts, and looked into them, their eyes should burst and their hands should wither and their hearts should rot.' This was surely 'beyond the limits of egocentricity', as Compton Mackenzie said of Lawrence's shout to him that there would not be another war. '*I* won't have another war.'

Paranoia was even more marked, more hysterically vocal, in his human relationships, and of all the friendships he had, and he had many, for his charm and sincerity were plain to see, not one escaped its violent quarrels. Even sagacious and tolerant Norman Douglas, even Mackenzie himself, did not evade the inevitable sizzling bitterness of Lorenzo when they failed to find him a superman above the ordinary courtesies of life, and afterwards the mean little caricature in one of Lawrence's books was the certain outcome. 'Good friends he had and used them all for copy', and his books depend for their interest on groupings and regroupings of these friends from early Derbyshire to Italy, via Australia and Mexico, in many poses and combinations, in febrile love-affairs and meaningless adulteries.

I used the word paranoia in its popular rather than its rigidly clinical sense, but it fails to convey the obsessions of a man who had no interest but himself. In his aspiring adolescence he could join no political or any other kind of party, could belong to no movement, take part in no activity in which he was not the bear-leader, so in later life he hurriedly dropped everything, or everyone, if he was not recognized as a demigod. The colony he was to found—a recurrent masturbatory dream—never in the end took shape, because its inhabitants to be, though they were changed again and again in Lawrence's mind, could not be visualized by him for long enough in sufficiently reverential positions. It would not have mattered if he could have seen incipient rebellion in their eyes, for he wanted his crucifixion as well as his hosannas, but he foresaw with the mad shrewdness of the schizophrenic that Lorenzo might be—not betrayed or sacrificed but treated with indifference or petty ridicule, and that was too much for him.

No interest but himself; it is an appalling summary yet nearly true. He loved landscape and described it most tellingly in his hammerstroke pleonastic prose, but all landscape was a backcloth for him. He looked out, he observed, he was moved by, he detested—every scene he painted is distorted by his own gesticulating figure in the foreground. He wrote of books but one could hear his voice—which even his most adulatory disciples have remembered as rasping—while he expounded invidiously. He wrote of people but his characters are all himself or someone he had known, or a mixture of the two, and his situations are all his own experiences, or the experiences he sought or feared. In all his work, in all his life, nothing was seen with detachment, nothing was considered, which did not affect him, *him* the godlike Lorenzo.

This gave to his work a certain strength. Within the limits of that egomania, which bounded his world like an immovable horizon, he achieved some powerful effects. His prose was repetitive and clumsy but he forced it to do his work. His people were faint tracings from his own malicious caricatures or idealized visions of himself, but by the energy of his phthisic lungs he breathed a sick life into them and made them move to

[173]

his will. His ideas were hallucinogenetic, his theories cloudy and ephemeral, but they were enough to resemble imagination and to deceive a million or two of readers over the years. As a writer he was an intellectual confidence-trickster who had long since persuaded himself and easily persuaded others.

4

This was the man, or the core of the man, who four years before his early death set out to write *Lady Chatterley's Lover*, remembering that a revered critic had said to him in his youth: 'I should welcome a description of the whole act.' 'It is,' he wrote, 'a phallic novel, but tender and delicate. You know I believe in the phallic reality, and the phallic consciousness: as distinct from our irritable cerebral consciousness of today. That's why I do the book—and its not just *sex*. Sex alas is one of the worst phenomena of today: all cerebral reaction, the whole thing worked from mental processes and itch, and not a bit of the real phallic insouciance and spontaneity.'

So he started with yet another dream-world from which he was excluded by his sterile intellectuality, as he was excluded from the 'aristocratic' world he named and jealously despised. This dream-world had been glimpsed from afar in earlier novels, a preposterous place where muscular peasants with 'loins' were moved by uncomplicated desires to 'phallic insouciance and spontaneity', a world very far removed, if it had existed, from Lawrence's own frenetic tubercular sexuality of mind, his own deepening impotence. From that world he drew his satyr, the gamekeeper Mellors, while his ravished and exultant victim he seduced from the abhorred 'upper classes' to humiliate her palsied husband. That would be the story, and

[*174*]

the whole story—the rest would be graphic and gushing 'phallicism'.

So it was. But Mellors was more than a satyr—he soon became the supreme example in Lawrence's work of the ideal Lorenzo. He is several kinds of wish-fulfilment. A few years younger than his creator he has the same red moustache and 'thick, almost fair' hair. His eyes at first are 'distant' and have a 'perfect, fearless, impersonal' look. Connie 'saw in his blue impersonal eyes a look of suffering and detachment', and felt a little shy of his 'curious, far-seeing eyes'. But we soon see 'those blue all-seeing eyes of his' which look 'warm and kind, particularly to a woman, wonderfully warm, and kind, and at ease'. On the next page the eyes are 'smiling again, a little mockingly, but warm and blue and somehow kind ... When his eyes ceased to laugh they looked as if they had suffered a great deal, without losing their warmth'. Further, a faint smile of mockery narrows them, they are 'quick', they have a 'cold ugly look of dislike and contempt', they are 'wicked blue' and 'keen blue', they 'go dark quite dark, the pupils dilating', they are 'tense and brilliant, fierce, not loving', 'blue', and 'with the flicker of irony'. But as other organs are brought into play these optical exercises are no longer recorded.

Mellors has the best of both worlds at his command. He is a miner's son who speaks the broad dialect of Derbyshire, but he can drop this in a moment to become an ex-officer and gentleman. He can not only express his scorn for his employers and their friends, he can, at the drop of a hat, become one of them. 'He had been an officer for some years and had mixed among the other officers and civil servants with their wives and families ... ' 'So he had come back to his own class. To find there, what he had forgotten during his absence of years, a pettiness and vulgarity of manner extremely distasteful.'

Physically he was a most remarkable animal, with 'curious

[*175*]

swift yet soft movements, as if keeping invisible'. 'He might almost be a gentleman. Anyway he was a curious, quick, separate fellow, alone but sure of himself.' 'He was rather frail really. Curiously full of vitality, but a little frail and quenched.' His face 'changed all the time, baffling'. 'In his shirt, without the clumsy velveteen coat, she saw again how slender he was, thin, stooping a little. Yet as she passed him there was something bright in his fair hair and his quick eyes.' 'He was naked to the hips, his velveteen breeches slipping down over his slender loins. And his white back was curved over a big bowl of soapy water ... She saw the clumsy breeches slipping down over the pure, delicate white loins, the bones showing a little. . . Perfect, white, solitary nudity of a creature that lives alone, and inwardly alone. And beyond that, a certain beauty of a pure creature. Not the stuff of beauty, not even the body of beauty, but a lambency, the warm, white flame of a single life, revealing itself in contours that one might touch: a body!' A body indeed, and the rest of the book does little but record its coy or boastful, its assertive or grimly playful 'phallic insouciance and spontaneity'.

Had Lawrence *no* sense of humour? Not a flicker to lighten all these pages of humdrum 'phallicism'? In his own life, as recorded by a number of admirers or detractors, there is no sign of it. He once wrote of his story *A Modern Lover* 'very comical, I think', and of *The Captain's Doll* 'a very funny long story'. A messianic conception of oneself leaves little room for humour and when that messianic conception is incarnated in Mellors he must never, even in bed, even in London (where he dressed 'in a formal suit of thin dark cloth' and 'could go anywhere' as he had 'a native breeding'), even in playful moments with Connie, be for a moment ridiculous.

There are the materials of this book, a shoddy little plot to cock a snook at the upper classes, an idealized out-of-category

[*176*]

Lorenzo figure given scope for concupiscence, and some minor characters sketched in pier artist's crayons, five shillings for a good likeness, the whole accompanied by rat-a-tat conversation of wearisome insignificance. From these Lawrence made his novel and thirty years after his death an English court solemnly debated its merits, sworn to by experts, and decided to allow its publication, while an ex-policeman edited the minutes of the trial to make another book. If Lawrence could not make his readers laugh he has certainly had the laugh on posterity.

5

Lady Chatterley's Lover is not pornography. It might have been better if it was. Written with earnest intent, written soberly with only an occasional lickerish snigger, it is, as witnesses maintained, a serious book, quite different from those jolly bits of bawdy description printed abroad, which have no purpose but to amuse and excite.

I was privileged once to hear from the author of one of the most famous of these, a book since taken quite seriously as a 'new departure' if not a 'masterpiece' in England, how it was put together. The publisher, realizing the vagaries of temperament and habit in his authors, paid them for piece-work, a thousand words a time. The author would appear at the office with his pages of typescript and the publisher would read them at once to see that they conformed to the required standard of 'juiciness'. If so, he handed over a small sum in cash; if not, he required enlivening revision before paying. This ensured a splendid standard of crowded pornography, for not a page could be written without something to excite jaded glands. Humour was not taboo and no 'message' was expected. Just plain dirt.

The system worked admirably as may be gathered from examples smuggled home by returning continental travellers.

That *Lady Chatterley's Lover* would have been a less stifling, and long-drawn-out affair written in this way can scarcely be doubted. For its four-letter words are its heart and guts. Idly, when I had finished it, I began paring away all the dead wood, all the mincing conversations between the guests at Wragby, all Clifford's rages, all the gossip of Mrs Bolton, all the wearisome descriptions of Connie's body and the fox-like physique of Mellors, all the tittering over-sexual intimacies, and what was left? Alas, nothing but the four-letter words, stark and shocking and slightly absurd. A trivial, tiresome book for vapid teenagers, as inoffensive as *Peter Pan*.

14

HOME PORT

As the little ship came into the western Mediterranean she began to buck and toss, and a howling rainstorm swept her decks. After a time she seemed to pitch with a sort of rhythm, each dive increasing to a fifth or sixth, a great burrowing dive with a hollow sensation in its depth, as though the ship had struck something beneath her. All night this continued and the bunk seemed to rise and fall as steeply as the ship, as though it shifted the stomach's weight towards head and feet alternately.

It was by the merest chance that I was to read Conrad to this highly appropriate motion of the sea. I find any attempt to read a book in its own setting sentimental and affected, an occupation for the worst kind of Victorian honeymoons. And in any case the book I had, *Nostromo*, was not a sea-story at all, though it was ostentatiously sub-titled 'A Tale of the Seaboard'. It was a story of an imaginary revolution in an imaginary state of South America, taking place, one presumes (though no dates are given), in the seventies or eighties of the last century, a too-neglected period for the modern novelist.

[*179*]

Here again I find that to gain all that may be gained from this novel one must glance back at the man who wrote it and the circumstances in which it was written. There are few novels for which this is a commendable practice, I think, and altogether too much is made of the lives of certain novelists like the Brontës. But *Nostromo* has a quality of something not written but created whole. Like the greatest music, one cannot easily conceive of it in manuscript. Yet of course it was, and very painfully so.

The story of Conrad's life can be reduced to a few bare dates and facts, as in each of his novels there is the dry skeleton of an old-fashioned plot deeply enveloped in the shining tissue of his prose. He was born in the Ukraine in 1857, the son of a volatile Polish patriot and man-of-letters named Apollo Korzeniowski and Evelina Bobrowski, member of a more staid Polish family. His mother died when he was seven, his father when he was eleven, both of tuberculosis. He was brought up by his maternal uncle, a kind, pompous, conscientious man, but at seventeen Conrad 'ran away to sea' or rather went, with a small allowance from his uncle, to Marseilles and from there made two voyages to the West Indies, first as a passenger, then as a member of the crew. He may have been involved in gun-running for the Carlists; certainly as a Pole liable for Russian military service he was no longer able to sail with the French and joined a British ship bound for Constantinople on which he came to Lowestoft and London in 1878. He learned English, took his Mate's and afterwards Master's Certificate and with one interval when he worked for a Belgian company in the Congo, remained in the British Merchant Service for sixteen years, serving mostly in the East. In 1894 his first novel *Almayer's Folly* was accepted for publication and in 1896 he married 'an inconspicuous little person' named Jessie George, by whom he was to have two sons. For twenty years, until the publication

[*180*]

of *Chance* brought him some financial success, he worked in anxiety, poverty and ill-health. For his last ten years, till his death in 1924, poverty alone of his misfortunes was relieved.

Conrad has always eluded his critics and biographers, who state a great many truths about him and his work but do not succeed in presenting him without the spectral mist behind which, though unwillingly, he worked and existed. The latest and most conscientious of writers on the subject, Mr Jocelyn Baines, in a lengthy critical biography *Joseph Conrad* (1960), gives us a mass of valuable detail from sources old and new, meticulously documented and surveyed with honest detachment, yet at the end of it Conrad, like his own Lord Jim, 'passes away under a cloud, inscrutable at heart'.

The mystery, or rather the miracle of his individual and highly coloured style has been a source of wonder since it first became known that his books were the work of a Pole who knew no English till his twenty-first year. The courage with which he planned his long novels and with agonizing difficulty fought his way to their completion, to be rewarded by inadequate payment and often uncomprehending criticism, is no less miraculous, though it has more precedents. But the real miracle, as with every great artist, is that he should have existed at all, that from the long ranks of humanity, contentedly undergoing the drill of existence, there should now and again step out an individual who volunteers to sacrifice himself for something which he may never earn the right to call his art.

For Conrad the sacrifice was a particularly heavy one. Born to parents for whom the cause of a free Poland meant everything, Conrad knew of his father's exile and his uncle's death in the service of that cause, and to the end of his life seems to have been nagged by a half-conscious remorse, a never-admitted fear, that he had been guilty of betrayal in preferring the sea and literature, which in him became almost one, to his duty as a

[*181*]

patriot. The theme of betrayal and atonement repeats itself in his novels; in *Lord Jim* and *Under Western Eyes* it is the main theme, and in *Nostromo* it is implicit in the stories of Nostromo himself and Dr Monygham. Conrad abandoned Poland for the sea and the sea for story-telling and in times of doubt of his own abilities he seems to have felt that he had abandoned an ideal for a shadow.

He made, too, the sacrifices common to most writers, of the consolation of action and direct experience which become emasculated by habits of observation and the need to interpret, of gusto, material prosperity, security, good health, the comfortable pettiness of conventional life. In all this he had little to sustain him but his own faith in his powers and that of a few friends and critics. 'I am conscious of having pursued with pain and labour a calm conception of a definite ideal in a perfect soberness of spirit.' At times this confidence in himself was high, at other times, particularly of illness, economic crisis or domestic stress, it was shattered. 'It appears to me that I will never write anything worth reading.'

The years in which Conrad was writing *Nostromo: A Tale of the Seaboard*, that is to say 1902 to 1904, were among the most difficult of his life. His connection with *Blackwood's Magazine* which had been a modest standby in bad times was (quite amicably) severed and a grant of £300 from the Royal Literary Fund did little but pay his more pressing debts. His wife became partially crippled and his banker, who had been his friend, failed, leaving Conrad with the necessity of paying off an overdraft. To his agent he wrote: 'I daren't draw a cheque. But I felt too sick of everything to write to you before. Moreover, my salvation is to shut my eyes and ears to everything—or else I could not write a line. And yet sometimes I can't forget—I remember the tradesmen, and all the horrors descend upon me.' To John Galsworthy: 'I didn't write to you because, upon my word, I am ashamed to write to anybody. I feel myself strangely growing into a sort of outcast. A mental and moral outcast. I hear nothing—I think of nothing—I reflect upon nothing—I cut myself off—and with all that I can just only keep going, or rather keep on lagging from one wretched story to another—and always deeper in the mire.' To David Meldrum, in December 1903: 'It has been a most disastrous year for my work. If I had written each page with my blood I could not feel more exhausted at the end of this twelvemonth.'

These letters, and many more as despairing, were written while *Nostromo* grew to its stately architectural proportions. Conrad had planned it as a short story 'belonging to the *Karain* class of tales'. He had hoped in March 1903 to finish it in three months and if he could do so, he told Ford Madox Hueffer, he would be 'saved for a time'. But his conception of the novel grew and very soon he must have realized where it was taking him, though even when he had written more than forty thousand words he told Galsworthy that the book, which eventually reached the total of nearly two hundred thousand words, was 'half done'.

The irresistible comparison in this respect is with *Don Quixote* which was also started as a novelette and written in poverty and ill-health with no security of any reward when its full purpose had been realized and fulfilled. But *El Ingenioso Hidalgo Don Quijote de la Mancha* is a picaresque work, never too carefully planned so that in reading of the Knight's misadventures we have the feeling that they are the week-to-week inventions of Cervantes. But *Nostromo* rises like a great building, every pilaster in place, as though constructed from a highly finished model.

In its spaciousness, in the grand scale of its composition, in its filigree detail, it is the last book one would expect from a harassed writer trying to make some money urgently needed for the maintenance of his family. Such a one might write a long novel, but it would be rambling and inconsequent, or a short book minutely planned. A continent and country mapped, painted in to the last scenic detail, given a full and very vivid history; a cast of some score of well-observed characters involved in a plot of remarkable complexity—these would surely be found only in the leisurely work of a novelist unvexed by immediate anxieties. Yet they came from this penurious neurasthenic who was writing in his letters at the time—'The question is—Can I make the effort —is it in me?' 'I have begun to write a good rate for a sick man.' 'To work in the conditions which are, I suppose, the outcome of my character mainly, is belittling—it is demoralizing.' 'I've been ill again. Just got down, shaky, weak, dispirited. No work done. No spring left to grapple with it. Everything looks black, but I suppose that will wear off, and anyhow, I am trying to keep despair under. Nevertheless I feel myself losing my footing in deep waters. They are lapping about my lips. My dear fellow it is not so much the frequency of these gout attacks, but I feel so beastly ill between, ill in body and mind. It has never been so before. Impossible to write—while the brain riots in incoherent images. It is sometimes quite alarming.' And when the book was at last finished: 'Phoo! I am weary. For more than a month I have been sitting up till three a.m.—ending with a solid 36 hours (in the middle of which I had to wire for the dentist and have a tooth drawn!!...) It broke!!...!! Till at 11.30 *I* broke down just after raising my eyes to the clock. Then I don't know; two blank hours during which I must have got out and sat down— (not fallen) on the concrete outside the door. That's how I found myself; and crawling in again noted the time; considerably after one. But I've finished. There's no elation. No relief even. Nothing. Moreover I've yet a good fortnight's work for the book form ... I am weary! weary.'

There is nothing hurried or makeshift about the planning of

Nostromo, or in any important respect about its execution. But in the text of the first edition there are signs of Conrad's frantic impatience to be done with it, his resentment at that 'good fortnight's' work needed to prepare the manuscript for press. As it appeared from 'Harper and Brothers of London and New York' in 1904 it has a number of misprints; dozens, and if we count wrongly accented words, scores of mistakes in Spanish. A word will appear in italics on one page and in Roman type on the next.

It is strange that neither the author nor the publisher should have had the proofs read by someone with at least a rudimentary knowledge of Spanish, which Conrad had not. *Jefe*, which is unaccented, appears as Jéfé, Jefé, Gefé and once even—an obvious misprint—pefé. 'Pepe' which also should be unaccented comes throughout as Pépé and many words that require accents are without. Conrad writes *intrada* for *entrada*, *ranche* for *rancho*, *pays* for *país* and makes countless other small mistakes which could easily have been corrected. Less trivial is a blunder which shows how much he depended on his reading for the authenticity of his background. In Argentina and Chile, and probably other countries, the South American Indians, who are of Mongolian origin and appearance, are known as *chinos*. Conrad speaks of 'the China girls' at the Violas' house, and later, presumably referring to the same, 'the Indian girls'. These things, unimportant in themselves, make the book's exact and scrupulous construction and writing the more remarkable.

John Galsworthy wrote of *Nostromo* that it was Conrad's 'most sheer piece of creation' and Richard Curle said that Conrad's power of visualization was immense. 'For example, he built up the whole atmosphere of *Nostromo*, which breathes the very spirit of South America, from a few days upon the coast.' From these legitimate criticisms and from others less informed it has often been inferred that *Nostromo* was the most

[*185*]

remarkable feat of the imagination which Conrad achieved. It may be so, but not because in it Conrad created a seaboard city, a range of mountains and a population with such extraordinary visual clarity that he transports the reader to his setting. To suggest that is to put a low value on imagination, or to over-simplify it to mean, as it did in childhood, merely the power to see with the mind's eye. *Nostromo*, set in a fictitious country of a continent on which Conrad had been ashore for only a day or two, is on that account neither more nor less 'creative' than *Lord Jim* which takes place against a background he knew. To say so is to suggest that *Romeo and Juliet* is a greater feat of crea-tion than *King Henry IV* because the scene of the latter was familiar to Shakespeare.

This is true also of the characters. These, so far as has been traced, owe little to Conrad's acquaintances in the past. For Kurtz of *Heart of Darkness* there was a prototype named Klein whom Conrad met in the Congo; in *Youth* even the names of the captain and mate, Beard and Mahon, are of men under whom Conrad had served in his first voyage as second officer in a ship called the *Palestine* (changed to *Judea* in the story). Conrad him-self, in his Author's Note to *Victory* says that he came on 'Mr Jones' in the West Indies and 'Ricardo' in the Gulf of Mexico. The events of *Lord Jim* are certainly based on the history of a pilgrim ship called the *Jeddah* and Jim himself may owe some-thing to the character of a certain Jim Lingard. But the people of *Nostromo*, so far as we know, have been whistled up from nothing, are out of the blue, as one may fairly say.

An author's sources are his own affair and it detracts in no way from the 'creativeness' of Shakespeare that his plots were drawn from Holinshed's Chronicles or that he had known a Justice Shallow. Sources are interesting but wholly irrelevant to a consideration of the merits of a book. Conrad himself was usually secretive about them. In his Author's Note to *Nostromo*

he says that the first hint for it came to him from an anecdote he
had heard while in the Gulf of Mexico in 1875 or 1876 and that
he had later read an account of the single-handed theft of a
lighter full of silver by a seaman in some memoirs bought in a
second-hand bookshop. Mr Jocelyn Baines, quoting with per-
mission an article unpublished when he wrote in 1959, by Mr
John Halverson and Professor Ian Watt of the University of
California, is able to identify this book as *On Many Seas: the
Life and Exploits of a Yankee Sailor* by Frederick Benton
Williams, edited by his friend William Stone Booth. In this
a crude form of the central incident of *Nostromo* is recounted.
Mr Baines adds that 'in view of this and of Conrad's tendency to
disguise his indebtedness to books, his claim to have heard the
anecdote himself in the Gulf of Mexico must be treated with
circumspection'. It has also been pointed out that Conrad must
have studied George Frederick Masterman's *Seven Eventful
Years in Paraguay* from which he took the names Gould,
Decoud, Corbelan, Mitchell, Fianza, Barrios and Monygham.
Conrad had also read Edward B. Eastwick's *Venezuela* in which
are found a number of geographical features, names and people
which he used.

Such information is of fascinating interest to the student of
Conrad's methods but for his readers it has very little significance. Conrad created the Republic of Costaguana, the Golfo
Placido, the town of Sulaco and all the people who live in this
novel, and it matters not at all that he used existing names for
them or that in presenting his characters he may have had in
mind some man with whom he had sailed, some woman
glimpsed in a Venezuelan street or some ruffian first encoun-
tered in the pages of a book. 'Male and female created he them',
and breathed into them life as he knew it. He certainly gave
them such reality of appearance that we see each of them as a
separate portrait, even to the miners—'the heads of gangs,

N   [*187*] distinguished by brass medals on their bare breasts'. Those brass medals might serve as a symbol of the futility of too much source-hunting. Somewhere, it may be, Conrad had read of, or perhaps seen such a foreman's mark on a miner, or he may have invented it himself. What does it matter? It gives a small touch of authenticity to the scene and that is enough.

The distinction of *Nostromo* from Conrad's other novels does not lie in its being his 'most sheer piece of creation', though visually this may be true. It lies in its enormous scope and in the manner of its presentation. Conrad hitherto had been concerned with the individual, or with the individual's concern with the individual. Here he takes a diversity of creatures and sets them against running history, makes them a part of the public life of a disturbed country, gives them, in every instance, a part to play in the affairs of that country.

Since at the same time Conrad could not lose his concern with his characters as individuals, the scope of the thing became enormous. As usual he spends most time with those who obstinately refuse to come to life and gives many pages to an attempt to animate Charles Gould. But with the background, the prodigious plot, the universal application, the running together of threads and the steady rise in temperature of the book, there comes a point at which it is in danger of growing to impossible dimensions and losing its coherence. It towers up, climax upon climax, until like its own Higuerota, its outlines seem to be losing themselves in the clouds.

At this point, when Conrad might have lost control, have been crushed by his own monstrous creation, he shows his superbly cool mastery of it. With characteristic wiliness he does not bring the story to the highest peak of its natural climax but leaving it there among the clouds, lets its events be told retrospectively by the sturdy and rather pompous Captain Mitchell from a point of comparative calm, which however precedes the final denouement. This brilliant stroke leaves the proportions of the book unimpaired.

Conrad had found in *Youth*, *Lord Jim*, *Heart of Darkness* the method best suited to the presentation of intensely subjective studies of men confronted with moral dilemma or the hostile forces of nature. He had created Marlow to stand between author and reader to interpret and intensify the story, to give it point and subtlety and reality which the author as an objective historian, supposedly without prejudices or emotions, could not do. It was a method well adapted to Conrad's genius and if he had learned to use it when he began *The Rescue* it would not perhaps have taken him more than twenty years and a number of false starts and blind alleys before he could at last finish that book. But for *Nostromo* as he saw it, 'more of a novel pure and simple than anything else I've done since *Almayer's Folly*', the method was impracticable. He wanted Costaguana to be presented by an historian and geographer and its people directly by their creator rather than by an observer involved in their affairs.

Objectivity, however, was impossible to him for long and we are continually watching the characters in *Nostromo* not as they appeared to the world at large or to their impersonal chronicler but as they are discussed or considered by other characters. Nostromo himself first appears as the Violas know him, the Goulds in the eyes of the engineer-in-chief of the railway, and so on. Moreover, twice in the book the objective method breaks down altogether. Martin Decoud—quite incredibly if one must be bound by circumstantial probability—spends a night of crisis in his own life and that of Sulaco in writing to his sister in Paris a letter of some eight thousand words in which we see people and events as this young man saw them. Later, when the revolution is over, Captain Mitchell recalls its events as seen by himself, a very different observer.

These are no more than technical contrivances in *Nostromo*, not to be compared with Marlow's appraisals at the length of a complete novel, but they show how reliant Conrad had become on this manner of presentation through the supposed discernment of another.

He cannot—it would be fairer to say that he did not wish to achieve complete objectivity, but in *Nostromo* he comes nearer to it than in any other novel. There is a marked scarcity, too, of those philosophical diversions, those oblique scrutinies of motive, those devices to give greater intimacy to the story which he used with such effect elsewhere. Yet the verbiage is truly Conradian and those to whom his curious, thoughtful and on the whole effective use of English words to define or pinpoint the intricacies of his meaning is essential for the enjoyment of Conrad will not be disappointed here. Too often instead of elucidation his phrases produce a coloured mist through which his characters are glimpsed about their nebulous purposes, but to the Conradian that mist, with its suggestion of the eternal ambiguities, is as precious as his sudden piercing of it to show stark outlines and incisive meanings when he wishes.

Mrs Gould saw the 'first spungy lump of silver yielded to the hazards of the world' and laid 'unmercenary hands' on it. When the Dictator came on board, 'the mirthless smile of his dark lips and the sightless glitter of his spectacles could be seen turning amiably from side to side', while the man who was to succeed him sat and 'the imbecile and domineering stare of the glorious victor of Rio Seco had in them something ominous and incredible; the exaggeration of the cruel caricature, the fatuity of solemn masquerading, the atrocious grotesqueness of some military idol of Aztec conception and European bedecking'. Guzman Bento had ruled the country with 'sombre imbecility'; 'usually full of fanciful fears and brooding suspicions'

[*190*]

he 'had sudden accesses of unreasonable self-confidence when he perceived himself elevated on a pinnacle of power and safety beyond the reach of mere mortal plotters', and he would 'scatter acts of political grace in a sardonic wantonness of clemency'. Father Corbelan 'remained quite motionless for a time with that something vengeful in his immobility which seemed to characterize all his attitudes. A lurid glow of strong convictions gave its peculiar aspect to the black figure'. A small boat is 'embraced' by 'a recrudescence of obscurity'. Sotillo turned away from Dr Monygham because 'he could bear no longer that expressionless and motionless stare, which seemed to have a sort of impenetrable emptiness like the black depth of an abyss'. His 'want of moral sense was a profound and inno-cent character'.

Is this over-writing? There is no standard of comparison for no one has used English as Conrad did. We look for such idiom and love it in his work and if in rare instance it overspills into fatuity the price is not too great to pay. *Nostromo* is magnifi-cently written and though sometimes Conrad uses too prodig-ally his characteristic vocabulary and imagery the effect is never overpowering and very rarely obscure.

The characterization achieved by Conrad differs from that of most other writers in its insistence on behaviour and motive rather than on some eccentricity or exaggerated quality of his subject. His are not the one-dimensional characters of Dickens, characters who act with a consistency which is at times absurd and at their lowest are little more than personified tricks of speech. Conrad creates his characters through their actions minutely observed by himself or one of his narrators, through their physiognomies and through their aims, which are often complicated, rather than through their narrated thoughts or even through their direct speech. He is not above a touch of caricature at times but usually he is preoccupied with subtleties

[*191*]

of action and reaction, with obscure causes and influences. His most successful full-scale creations like Jim, Almayer, Heyst, are formed by the same process as Hamlet and his minor ones bear more relationship to Jaques or Touchstone than to the small fry of Dickens.

In *Nostromo* there is, perhaps, no fully observed, deeply understood, four-dimensional character, though a great many people are shrewdly perceived and admirably portrayed. Mrs Gould, Dr Monygham, Nostromo himself (though in him the process seems a little laboured), Don Pepe, Decoud (treated with more fervent analysis), Captain Mitchell, Guzman Bento, Antonia Ribera, Jose Avellanos, Hirsch, old Viola and his wife, the Montero brothers, Colonel Sotillo and in less detail Gamacho and Fuentes and at the last Linda and Giselle—these are all people revealed, made comprehensible, people whom the reader 'gets to know' in the course of this novel. Others are as carefully attempted but less successful and Father Corbelan is an obsession in clerical garb, Charles Gould no more than a red moustache with a hobby-horse. But Conrad was not concerned here as in *Lord Jim* with the study of an individual in unhappy relation to his world. *Lord Jim* is a portrait with an exotic background; *Nostromo* is a landscape with figures.

In telling his story Conrad breaks all the rules of narrative. 'Begin at the beginning and go on till you come to the end: then stop', said Lewis Carroll wisely, but Conrad does none of these. After a scenic prelude the story begins with a day of revolt, returns to the time of uneasy peace which preceded it and thereafter the progression is chopped into passages sometimes reaching back to the past and sometimes into the future. The impression is of a man painting a vast mural of which only the thinnest outline has been drawn and concentrating his colours first here then in another corner till the whole is completed. It has even been suggested that the last two chapters are a melodramatic appendix, inadequately related to the body of the book But all this takes nothing from the story and I know of no great book which fills the reader with such greed to turn the page and see what happens next.

As the reader follows one after another of the false scents at the beginning of the book, he wonders what story Conrad means to tell, and when he regretfully reaches the end he may still feel some doubts. It is certainly not the story of Nostromo and his hidden treasure though that anecdote may first have set it in motion. 'Silver', wrote Conrad long after the publication of *Nostromo*, 'is the pivot of the moral and material events, affecting the lives of everybody in the tale.' That is well so far as it goes, though it would have to be strained to make it wholly true. Conrad also wrote of *Nostromo* that it was his ambition to 'render the spirit of an epoch in the history of South America', and if that was truly so, and truly all, he failed. Costaguana is not in any continent and the events of this book belong to no epoch, though it may be said, perhaps, that it is everywhere and its events of all time. For Costaguana is a country of the mind created not to 'render the spirit of an epoch' but, down to the last shaft of sunlight on its peaks or on the gold lace of its officials, as the setting for something which concerned Conrad more than epochs and continents, a splendid story of treachery and ambition, of greed and heroism, of some love and much hatred, and above all of the universal, highly entertaining, deeply moving futility of human endeavour.

2

As we neared Gibraltar the steward told me, in a manner which suggested that he was both impressed and somewhat amused, that we were calling there for the sole purpose of allowing me to disembark.

'And to drop some cigarettes,' I reminded him.

He shrugged.

'A dozen cases. Nothing. They could have waited.'

Harry Ingham, my fellow-passenger, was almost sceptical.

'I've never heard of a cargo boat calling at a port especially for one passenger,' he said.

It was, I was given to understand on all sides, a unique situation, and one which might have interested or perhaps exasperated the man whose book I had been reading. He and his fellow-seamen in the days of sail would have found it an unwarrantable piece of interference in the working of a ship by those ashore, owners or agents, and I have no doubt the Yugoslav Captain and his officers thought the same. The agent in Gibraltar afterwards told me that the ship's brief stop in the harbour had cost the Yugoslav Line considerably more than my two-way passage, for officials had to come out, documents be inspected, the ship delayed, port dues paid—not to mention several launches alongside.

But whoever had been interviewed in the huge rococo building occupied by Jugolinija in Rijeka had been all-powerful and my appeal to him had succeeded. I came ashore in the agent's launch with twelve cases of cigarettes and before I had reached the jetty the ship I had left weighed anchor. She looked regal in the spring sunshine and I felt as though I had halted a royal procession.

My voyages through the wintry sea were done and I have not boarded another ship or read a novel since that day.